The Human Body

Grades 4-6

Written by Vi Clarke and Leona Melnyk
Illustrated by Liz Mercz and Ric Ward

ISBN 1-55035-143-5
Copyright 1990
Revised October 2007
All Rights Reserved * Printed in Canada

Published in the United States by:
On The Mark Press
3909 Witmer Road PMB 175
Niagara Falls, New York
14305
www.onthemarkpress.com

Published in Canada by:
S&S Learning Materials
15 Dairy Avenue
Napanee, Ontario
K7R 1M4
www.sslearning.com

Look For Other Health & Safety Units

The Human Body

Table of Contents

The Human Body

Expectations

Students will:

- become more familiar with their body parts and how they function
- recognize and label diagrams of body parts
- become aware of the importance of nutritional eating and how it develops and benefits the body
- use vocabulary pertaining to the body correctly

Teacher Input Suggestions

1. **Planning Ahead:**

   Collect the following items prior to introducing and teaching the various parts of the human body: body part charts, diagrams of the human body, reference books, photographs (food, body parts, people in action) healthy foods, unhealthy foods, films, filmstrips, videos, CD-ROMS, web sites, slides, models of body parts such as the heart, lungs, teeth, brain, reproducible diagrams, Food Guides, health magazines, brochures

2. **Brainstorming:**

   Brainstorm words that pertain to the human body. Classify the words on charts entitled "Inside the Human Body" and "Outside the Human Body". Add to the charts as vocabulary surfaces during lessons. Words may also be classified on charts under the names of the different body systems. The lists may be used during spelling lessons and spelling games.

List of Vocabulary

acoustic, ambrosia, aorta, auricle, bicuspids, brainpan, calcium, cartilage, cerebrum, cerebellum, cholesterol, clairvoyance, clavicle, cochlea, cranium, cuspids, dentine, dermotoglyphics, dextrose, echolocation, encompass, femur, fibula, humerus, incisors, involuntary, magnesium, mandible, marrow, medulla, molars, myologist, olfactory, optometrist, palatable, patella, phalanx, plaque, potassium, precognition, psychokinesis, pulp, radius, redolent, retina, sternum, steroids, tarsals, telepathy, tendon, tibia, ulna, ventricle, voluntary

3. **Bulletin Board Displays:**

   a) Display poems that pertain to the human body around a picture of one.
   b) Place diagrams on the bulletin board for the students to label.
   c) Have a section of the bulletin board labeled Healthy Foods/Unhealthy Foods. The students may classify food pictures under the headings.

The Human Body

4. **Discussion Topics:**

The following topics may be discussed in any order. Find out how each system and its parts function. Discuss the importance of each one.

    a) The Skeletal System
    b) The Circulatory System
    c) The Brain
    d) The Muscular System
    e) The Teeth
    f) The Respiratory System
    g) The Digestive System
    h) Nutrition
    i) Care of the Body
    j) Major Diseases

5. Invite guest speakers such as a dental hygienist, doctor, nurse, nutritionist, dietician, optometrist, or anyone in the medical field to give presentations on health topics that the students may like to find out information about.

6. Discuss your Food Guide and have the students plan healthy meals and snacks.

List of Resources

Human Body Web Sites

Circulatory System: http://www.encyclopedia.com/articles/02772.html
http://www.fi.edu/biosci/heart.html

Digestive System: http://www.niggk.nith.gov/health/digest/pubs/digesyst/newdiges.htm
http://www.encyclopedia.com/articles/03656.html

Respiratory System: http://www.stemnet.nf.ca/ power/resp/struct 1.htm

General: http://sln.fi.edu/tfi/activity/act-summ.html
http://www.lessonplanspage.com/Science45.htm (Lesson Plans)

Videos: Bill NYE The Science Guy
Titles: Digestion, Blood, Circulation, Bones, Muscles, and Respiration

The Human Body

CD-ROMS

1. <u>A.D.A.M. The Inside Story '97 School Edition</u> is a multimedia introduction to the secrets of the human body. Explore the body layer by layer, then join modern day Adam and Eve as the body's miracles come alive with entertaining animations, video, and sound in their Family Scrapbook. Useful for grades five to eight.

This title was the winner of the 1996 Software Publishers Association "Codie" Award for "Best Education Product for Middle Schools" and "Best Curriculum-Based Education Product". It has won the Curriculum Administrators' Top 10 District Choice Award.

Highlights of this award-winning CD-ROM include:

- Over 4 000 individual structures can be identified as the human anatomy is revealed from skin to bone in hundreds of layers, seeable in anterior and posterior, lateral, and medial views.

- Animation, video, and sound detail normal and abnormal physiological processes.

- Quickly reference the glossary of anatomical terms, audio pronunciation, system reference text, or challenge your students with interactive anatomy puzzles.

- Rotate the 3-D anatomical images to identify important structures, then take an animated tour through each designated body part.

- The Quizmeister feature allows students to test their knowledge with a series of 12 multi-question quizzes.

- Print capabilities, Internet access, and supplemental detailed bank of images!

The combination of A.D.A.M.'s high-quality imagery and compelling "inside the body" approach to learning makes this title an invaluable tool for introductory study of the human body. It makes a great complement to any Anatomy and Physiology, Health, Physical Education, Human Biology or Health Career Class.

This product has a modesty setting that locks out the reproductive system and covers male and female genitals with "fig leaves".

Teacher's Guide:

Also included is a Teacher's Guide of curriculum integration activities to help educators for grades five through eight integrate the program into the classroom. Co-developed with educators and students, this guide contains anatomical system overview, interdisciplinary classroom activities with reproducible worksheets, summaries of the product's animations and videos, lists of key terms, and detailed illustrations for each system. The Teacher's Guide also includes innovative activities that reinforce science lessons through art. Teacher materials include ideas on managing computer resources in the classroom, working with special needs students, and a bibliography of additional reference sources.

The Human Body

2. **A.D.A.M.'s Award Winning Software** combines the Inside Story and Life's Greatest Mysteries in one package, <u>The Inside Story Complete</u>. Students will be entertained and challenged with this wonderful interactive learning tool. Teachers will enjoy how easy the integration into existing curriculum can be.

Fosters Academic Growth:

CD components (Inside Story, Anatomy, The Family Scrapbooks, Activities, Glossary, Images, Reference Text, Videos, and Animations) help meet challenges in problem solving, writing, math, spelling, and language arts and therefore foster academic growth in the teacher's guide.

Fostering Social Growth:

The materials invite small group work. Students working in teams can delegate roles, ask some team members to read aloud and others to record, research, and motivate. Team members can learn how to negotiate, delegate, solve problems, and recognize individual strengths.

Fosters Emotional Growth:

The interactive design encourages active learning that is self-paced and allows for self evaluation. The menu items offer choices that reflect sensitivity to students' interests in gender (female, male) and skin tone. Animation and video topics provide springboards for discussion about real-life issues such as smoking, choking, pregnancy, and exercise. All students have individual leaning styles. The multimedia format helps students with disabilities by presenting information through a variety of modalities simultaneously.

Life's Greatest Mysteries:

Mind, Body, Psyche CD Components include answers to mind, body, and psyche questions, while debunking myths and shattering illusions about the human body and mind, sickness, and curiosities.

Teacher's Guide:

The explicit learning objectives facilitate preparation of lesson plans and individualized education plans. Analogies and jingles offer mnemonic devices to aid in memorizing. Many teacher's guide activity worksheets and branches invite student teams to find several answers to the same question.

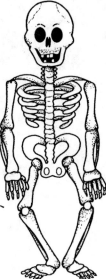

The Skeletal System

Activity One

"Bone" - y Terminology

How knowledgeable are you about "bone" - y terminology?

In the sentences that follow, see if you can fill in the blanks using the words located in the box at the bottom of the page.

Use resource books or a dictionary where necessary.

1. Strong bands that help to keep our bones in their proper place are called _____.

2. A _____ is the place where two bones come together and fit against one another.

3. A soft yellow or red substance found in the central cavities of the bones is called the _____.

4. The _____ is the only bone in the skull that moves.

5. If a bone breaks, the condition is known as a _____.

6. A small triangular bone at the end of the spine is known as the _____.

7. _____ are the tough connective tissues that fasten muscles to the bones.

---

jawbone, marrow, ligaments, coccyx, tendons, joint, fracture

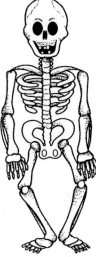

The Skeletal System

Activity Two

"Boning Up" on Information

Do some research and decide which of the three answers is the best one. All questions have to do with the skeleton - your body's framework.

Underline the correct answer.

1. How many red blood cells does bone manufacture every day?
   a) 500   **b)** 10 000   **c)** 1 000 000 000

2. How many bones are there in your body?
   a) 206   **b)** 300   **c)** 150

3. What is the main mineral found in bone?
   a) magnesium   **b)** calcium   **c)** potassium

4. Where are half of the body's bones located?
   a) in your arms and legs   **b)** in your hands and feet
   c) in your brain and spinal cord

5. What is the human skull made of?
   a) one bone   **b)** two bones joined together   **c)** 29 different bones

6. What is the shock absorber in your body?
   a) the knee   **b)** the elbow   **c)** the spine

7. Which bone is the strongest and heaviest of all the bones in your body?
   a) femur   **b)** tibia   **c)** fibula

8. Which bone is your "funny bone"?
   a) elbow   **b)** humerus   **c)** radius

9. Which bones form a kind of cage?
   a) ribs   **b)** pelvis   **c)** spine

10. What is the soft tissue called that fills the hollow or central part of most bones?
    a) cartilage   **b)** marrow   **c)** vitamins

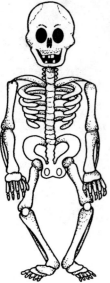

The Skeletal System

Activity Three

Mr. Skelly-Ton

Part A:

Below are the names of several bones in our body.

Match the bones with the appropriate body parts.

Then show where each bone is on "Mr. Skelly-Ton".

Consult an encyclopedia or other resource books and do some reading on the skeletal system prior to doing this activity.

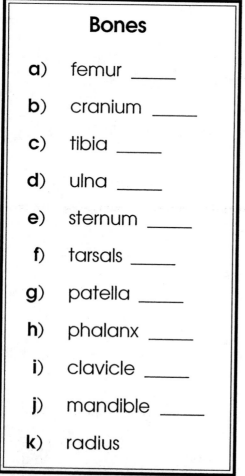

Bones
a) femur _____
b) cranium _____
c) tibia _____
d) ulna _____
e) sternum _____
f) tarsals _____
g) patella _____
h) phalanx _____
i) clavicle _____
j) mandible _____
k) radius

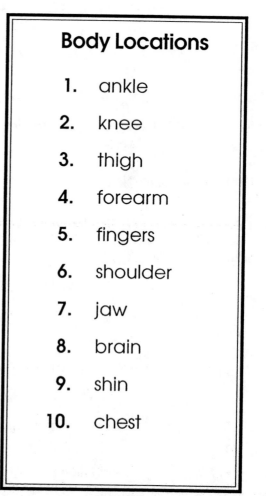

Body Locations
1. ankle
2. knee
3. thigh
4. forearm
5. fingers
6. shoulder
7. jaw
8. brain
9. shin
10. chest

OTM-402 • SSD1-02 The Human Body

The Skeletal System

Activity Three

Mr. Skelly-ton

Part B: Label the parts of your skeleton.

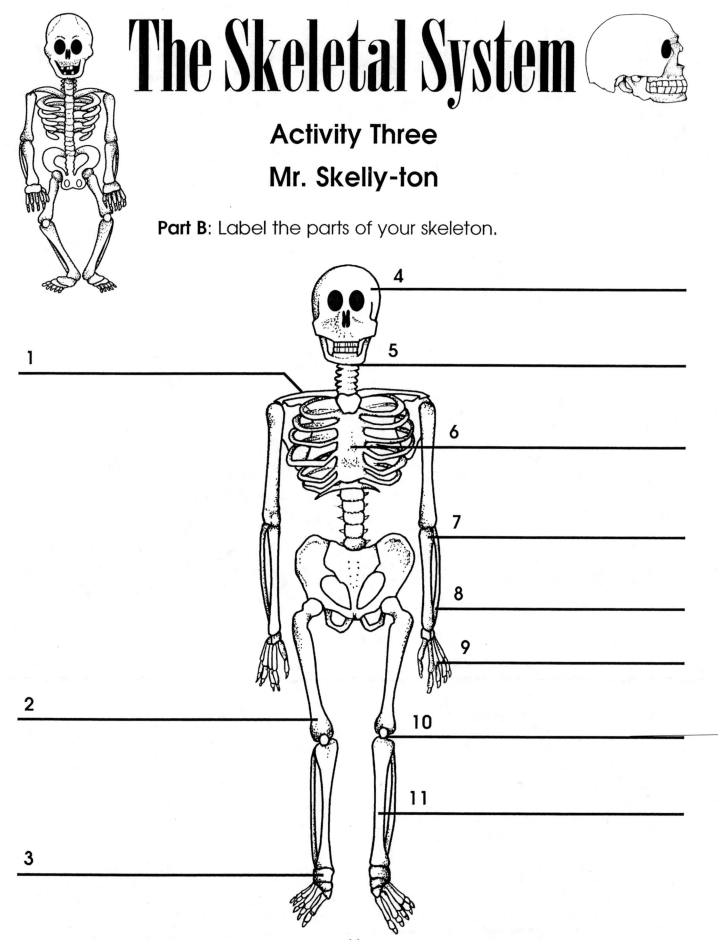

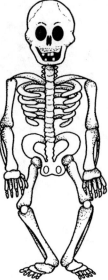

The Skeletal System

Activity Four

Skeleton Mystery

Using a pencil, shade in all the parts of the body that are the names of bones.

When you do, a hidden part of your body will appear.

Use a dictionary to help you.

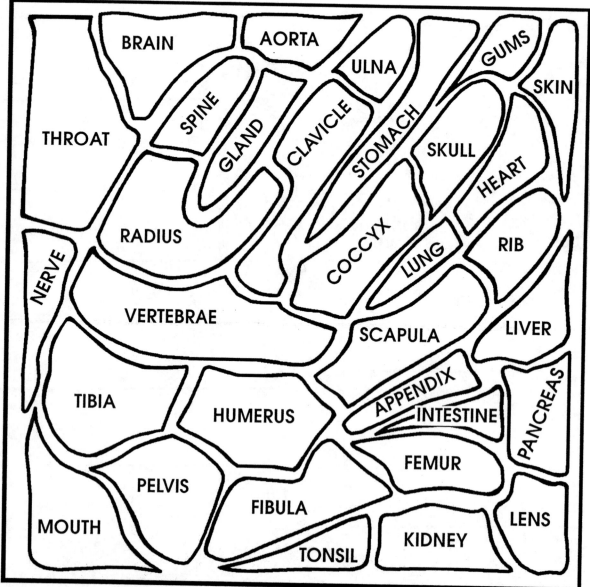

BRAIN · AORTA · ULNA · GUMS · SKIN · SPINE · GLAND · CLAVICLE · STOMACH · SKULL · THROAT · HEART · RADIUS · COCCYX · LUNG · RIB · NERVE · VERTEBRAE · SCAPULA · LIVER · TIBIA · HUMERUS · APPENDIX · INTESTINE · PANCREAS · FEMUR · PELVIS · FIBULA · LENS · MOUTH · KIDNEY · TONSIL

The Skeletal System

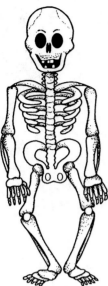

Activity Five

Body Sayings

Did you ever tell someone to "break a leg"?

Have you ever eaten something "finger-lickin' good"?

There are many sayings that make mention of some part of the body.

Copy and complete each saying with a body part.

1. She has a "green _____" because her plants grow well.

2. He's "_____ high to a grasshopper".

3. They lost the game by the "_____ of their teeth".

4. This steak is as "tough as _____".

5. I am so nervous that I have "butterflies in my _____."

6. "Cross my _____ and hope to die", I did not tell you a lie.

7. My little brother is such a "pain in the _____" when I have to babysit him.

8. The eerie sound frightened me and caused my "_____ to stand up on end".

9. What I said must have gone in "one _____ and then out the other".

10. His wife is so bossy that she "leads him around by the _____".

11. People who have something to hide about their past may have a "_____ in the closet".

12. His kind words about my father "warmed the cockles of my _____".

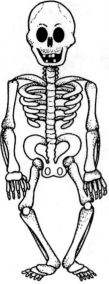

The Skeletal System

Activity Six

Math for Every-"body"

Locate a piece of string and a ruler so you and your body can do some math.

Answer the following questions:

1. Measure the distance from fingertip to fingertip of your outstretched arms. Now measure your height. How do these two measurements compare?

2. Is your nose as tall as your ear?

3. Which half of your body is longer? Measure from your head to your waist, then from your waist to your feet.

4. Measure the distance between your wrist and your elbow. Measure the length of your foot. How do they compare?

5. Does the distance from the base of your nose to the point of your chin equal the width of your hand?

How did you measure up? Are you surprised at the results? Do you think the measurements are the same for every body?

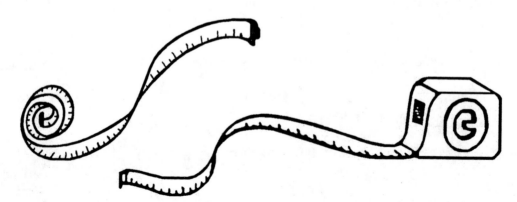

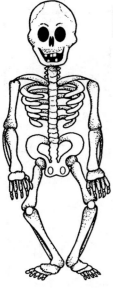

The Skeletal System

Activity Seven

Dermotoglyphics

How would you like to specialize in the study of dermotoglyphics?

What is dermotoglyphics?

Dermotoglyphics is the study of fingerprints.

Complete the following activities.

A) Research to find out the facts about fingerprints.

What are the three basic patterns?

What do they look like?

Write your findings in a proper paragraph.

B) Using a stamp pad, make your left and right thumb prints in the boxes provided.

Using similar squares of paper have ten of your classmates make two prints of their right thumb. Then gather the cards and have a game of "Concentration". See who can gather the largest number of matches. The winner will be a very perceptive person indeed!

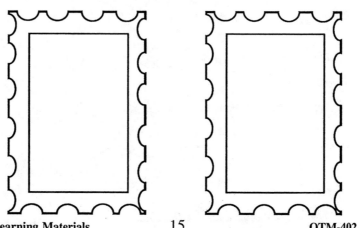

The Skeletal System

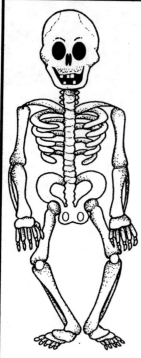

Activity Eight

A "Hip" - py Tune

Try your hand at making up a song about your "bones"!

I'm sure you recall the tune "The hip bone's connected to the thigh bone, the thigh bone's connected to the knee bone and so on....."

See what kind of a "hip" - py tune you can come up with.

Your lyrics could be sung to a familiar tune. Perhaps "Brother John!"

The Skeletal System

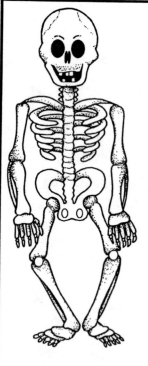

Activity Nine

Mr. Bones

Pencil a skeleton on black or dark blue construction paper.

Take a handful of wooden toothpicks.

Cut or break them into pieces.

Example:

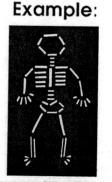

Glue them onto your sketch to make a bone-a-rific skeleton.

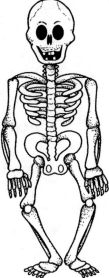

The Skeletal System

Activity Ten

Bone Up on Writing

A pitiful sight we would be if we were mere skeletons walking about the streets or dangling ominously from tree branches.

At Hallowe'en, the mere sight of these spindly creatures is a little unnerving.

What could happen if you could reverse this universal view of the skeleton?

What would happen if a skeleton man appeared in your backyard and he turned out to be a warm, loving bundle of bones?

How would you protect him?

What name would you give him? The Boney Man, Frank N. Stein or perhaps Mr. Skelly Ton?

How would you protect him?

Would you tell your parents and friends?

What opposition would you face?

What would the end result be?

How would your story turn out?

Bone up on writing and share your experience!

The Skeletal System

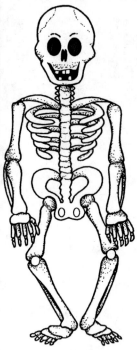

Activity Eleven

Bare Bones

From a piece of Bristol board, draw and cut out a model of a skeleton.

Attach the bones together with paper fasteners.

Label your skeleton with the names of bones.

Hang your skeleton in the classroom.

The Skeletal System

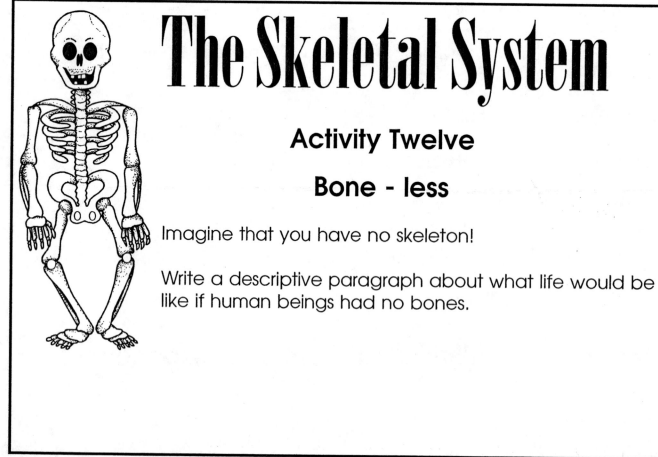

Activity Twelve

Bone - less

Imagine that you have no skeleton!

Write a descriptive paragraph about what life would be like if human beings had no bones.

The Skeletal System

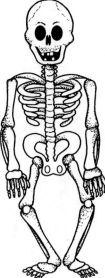

Activity Thirteen

Get Off on the Right Foot

Put your foot into this puzzle and try it on for size.

All you have to do is read the definitions and see how many compound words containing the word "foot" you can figure out.

Your dictionary may be required.

The number of lines tells you how many letters to use.

1. impression found in the sand   foot _ _ _ _ _ _
2. an insert at the bottom of a page   foot _ _ _ _
3. tired of walking   foot _ _ _ _
4. to be in someone's way   _ _ _ _ _ foot
5. boots and socks   foot _ _ _ _
6. servant or page   foot _ _ _
7. popular game   foot _ _ _ _
8. a boxer uses it   foot _ _ _ _
9. lying at the base of a mountain   foot _ _ _ _
10. for resting feet on   foot _ _ _ _ _
11. a new-comer   _ _ _ _ _ _ foot
12. hurry   _ _ _ foot
13. the sound made by a foot   foot _ _ _ _
14. used to cross water   foot _ _ _ _ _ _

The Skeletal System

Activity Fourteen

"Hands" - on Riddles

Who is the strongest man in the world?
(A policeman because he can hold up traffic with one hand.)

What did the left hand say to the other hand?
(It seems as if you are always right!)

Why do hands like to vacation in Hawaii?
(They like the palm trees there.)

Do these riddles make you smile?

Read a joke or riddle book in your resource center (library).

Copy **one** that tickles the funny bone or **write** one of your own.

Share your "hand"-picked favorite with a classmate.

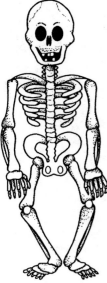

The Skeletal System

Activity Fifteen

Body Language

The following are common expressions that mention parts of the human body.

Do a little research and write the meaning for each one.

1. a skeleton crew _____

2. be on your toes _____

3. nothing but skin and bones _____

4. put your foot down _____

5. two heads are better than one _____

6. out of sight, out of mind _____

7. get off on the right foot _____

8. have one foot in the grave _____

9. it costs an arm and a leg _____

10. foot of the stairs _____

11. your inner self _____

12. a hard head _____

13. to have a bone to pick _____

14. hand over fist _____

The Skeletal System

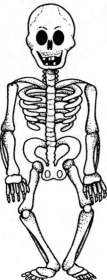

Activity Sixteen

An Unemployed Skeleton

Imagine that you are a skeleton who is presently unemployed.

You are browsing through the "Ghostly Daily News" when you happen upon a want ad.

Wanted!

Skeletons to appear in a new horror fiction

movie entitled "The Horror of Skeleton Cove".

Your opportunity to be a famous movie star.

Excellent wages and benefits. Experience

an asset. To arrange an interview, phone

Frank N. Stein Studios at 726 - GHOST.

Upon arrival at the studio you are requested to fill out the employee application form.

Complete the form on the next page.

 # The Skeletal System

Frank N. Stein Studios

Employee Application Form

1. Name: _____

           (Last)   (First)   (Middle)

2. Address: _____

3. Describe your job experiences (past haunting jobs, what you were expected to do and whether or not you were successful).

   _____

   _____

   _____

   _____

   _____

4. Have you had any courses in acting? If so, where? What are your favorite roles?

   _____

   _____

   _____

   _____

   _____

5. Do you have any special qualities as a skeleton actor? (For example, do you make any favorite scary, startling noises?)

   _____

   _____

   _____

   _____

   _____

The Brain

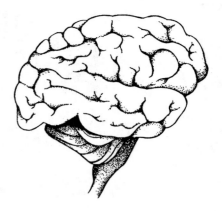

Activity One

Job Description

The brain occupies the entire top floor of the skull and from this lofty fortress it guides and controls you. The brain organizes the scattered parts of your body into one unit, makes you aware of things, and incites you to action.

The brain is divided into three sections:

1. the medulla

2. the cerebellum

3. the cerebrum

a) Do some research and write a job description telling what each part of the brain does.

b) Which is the busiest section of the brain?

c) Which is the largest part of the brain?

d) Label a diagram of the brain. Mark on the names of the three parts.

The Brain

Activity Two

The Centers of the Brain

Every second your brain receives and sorts out 100 million messages.

The messages come from your five senses: seeing, hearing, touching, smelling, and tasting.

On a diagram of the brain, show where the center of each of our senses is located.

There is also a speech center, a motor center from which messages are sent to the muscles, and a center for reasoning.

Can you label these centers as well?

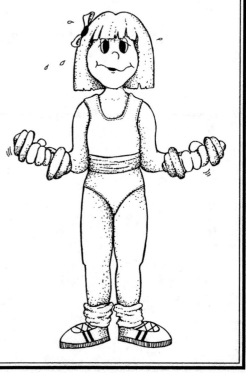

The Brain

Activity Three

Does This Make "Sense"?

Using the dictionary, find the meanings of the following words.

Then write the words under the proper headings on the picture of the brain to tell which of the five senses they are most likely associated with.

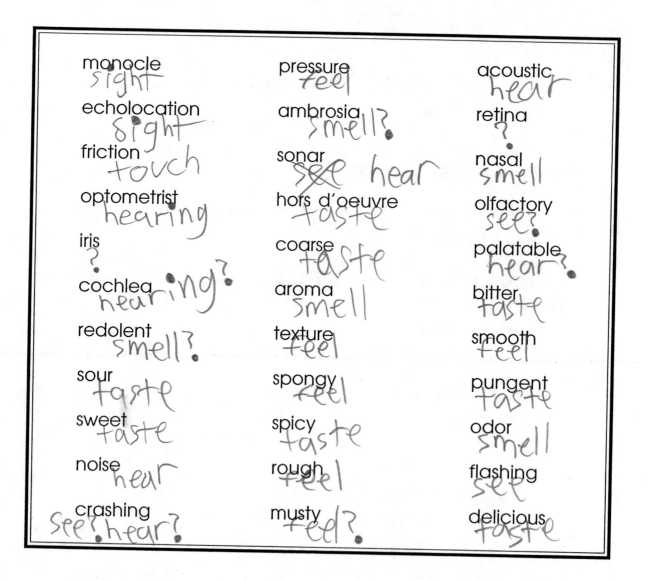

monocle *sight*

echolocation *sight*

friction *touch*

optometrist *hearing*

iris *?*

cochlea *hearing?*

redolent *smell?*

sour *taste*

sweet *taste*

noise *hear*

crashing *see? hear?*

pressure *feel*

ambrosia *smell?*

sonar *see hear*

hors d'oeuvre *taste*

coarse *taste*

aroma *smell*

texture *feel*

spongy *feel*

spicy *taste*

rough *feel*

musty *feel?*

acoustic *hear*

retina *?*

nasal *smell*

olfactory *see?*

palatable *hear?*

bitter *taste*

smooth *feel*

pungent *taste*

odor *smell*

flashing *see*

delicious *taste*

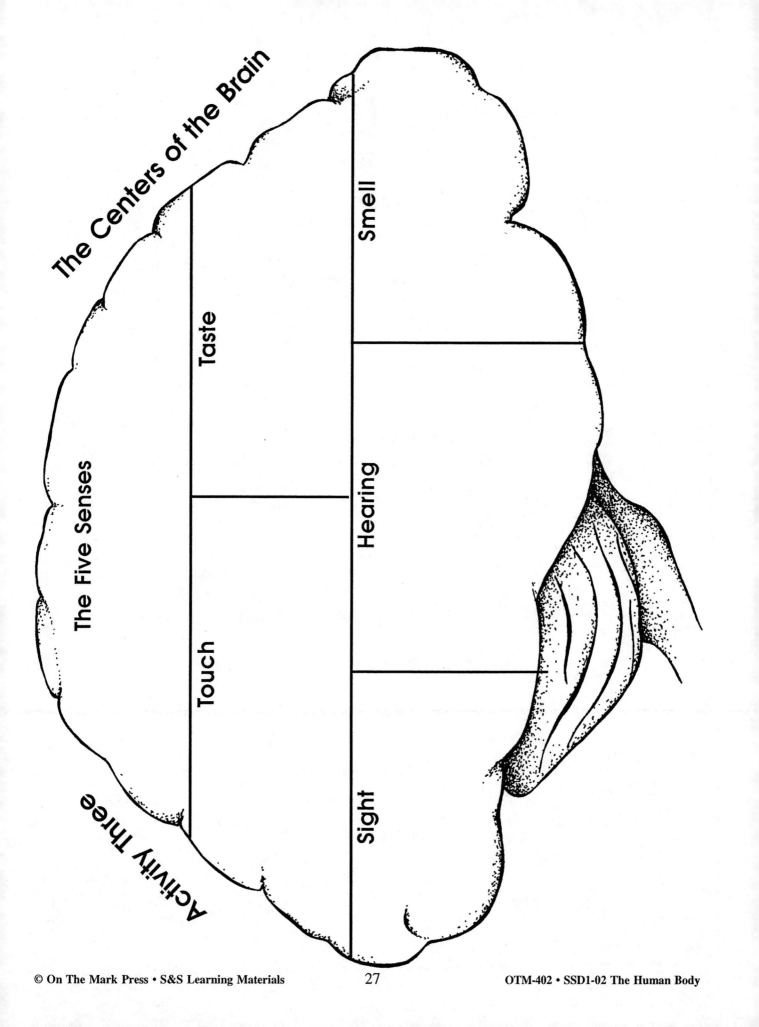

The Centers of the Brain

The Five Senses

Activity Three

Smell

Taste

Hearing

Touch

Sight

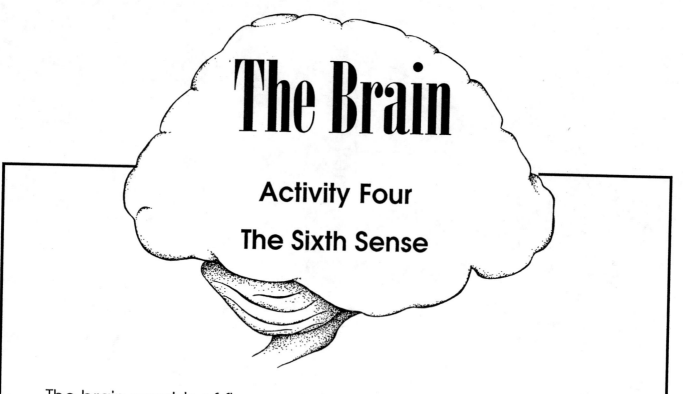

The Brain

Activity Four

The Sixth Sense

The brain consists of five sense areas:

- hearing
- seeing
- feeling
- smelling
- tasting

However, you may recall hearing about "the sixth sense".

Some people believe that we have extra senses that we are not aware of.

The sixth sense is better known as extrasensory perception or E.S.P.

There are different types of E.S.P.

To better understand this "extra" sense do some reading on the subject and write a sentence or two about the following types of E.S.P.

1. telepathy

2. psychokinesis

3. precognition

4. clairvoyance

The Brain

Exercise is vital – to brains as well as bodies. We must train the brain by challenging it with problems to think about and solve.

See how "brainy" you can be. Figure out these brain bogglers.

1. Use the numeral 8 three times in an equation to equal seven.

   Answer: _____

2. What 15 coins can you use to make a dollar?

   Answer: _____

3. Look at the following numerals. If you leave them in this order and insert only addition and subtraction signs, what will the equation be?
   1234567890 = 100

   Answer: _____

4. A farmer had 36 cows. All but 15 of them died. How many cows did the farmer have left?

   Answer: _____

5. At a horse race there were several horses and jockeys. If there were 82 feet and 26 heads, how many horses and how many jockeys were there?

   Answer: _____

6. Arrange 16 toothpicks to form this pattern. Remove 10 toothpicks so that you are left with only 2 triangles.

   Answer: _____

The Brain

Capitalizing on Brains

Copy the following sentences and supply all necessary capital letters and punctuation marks.

1. the brain is divided into three sections – the cerebrum the cerebellum and the medulla

   _____

   _____

   _____

2. the human brain is grayish-pink in color and weighs about 1.4 kilograms (three pounds)

   _____

   _____

   _____

3. the cerebrum weighs the most totaling 85 per cent of the 1.4 kilograms (three pounds)

   _____

   _____

   _____

4. shielding the brain from hard blows are hard bones called the cranium

   _____

   _____

   _____

5. the brain is at its full weight by the time a person is six years old

   _____

   _____

   _____

The Brain

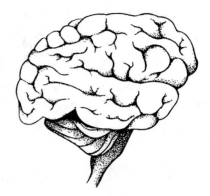

Activity Seven

"Brainy" Words

Fill in the blanks with the appropriate "brainy" words located in the box.
Use a dictionary to help you.

brain wave	brainwash	brain teaser
brainpan	brain drain	brain fever
brain child	brainless	brainstorm
brainy		

1. To alter one's beliefs by intense instruction is to _____.

2. A rhythmical fluctuating of the electrical power of the brain is known as a _____.

3. The cranium or skull is known as the _____.

4. An original idea or technique which someone creates is known as a _____.

5. To inspire and generate ideas is to _____.

6. The shortage of professional or skilled labor to other countries is called _____.

7. Someone who performs stupid or foolish acts is said to be _____.

8. Someone who is clever or very intelligent is often referred to as being _____.

9. A puzzle that tests a person's ability to reason is called a _____.

10. Meningitis or encephalitis are two types of _____ that can affect the human brain.

The Brain

Activity Eight

Great Minds

If you were able to choose from a gallery of geniuses, whose brain would you be interested in receiving?

Do some research on the following great minds of all times.

Choose one that interests you and pretend that you are that genius for a day.

Great Minds: Mozart   Rembrandt
                   Newton   Einstein
                   Da Vinci   Galileo

The Brain

Activity Nine

Brain Teasers

Give your mind a workout by solving these brainteasers.

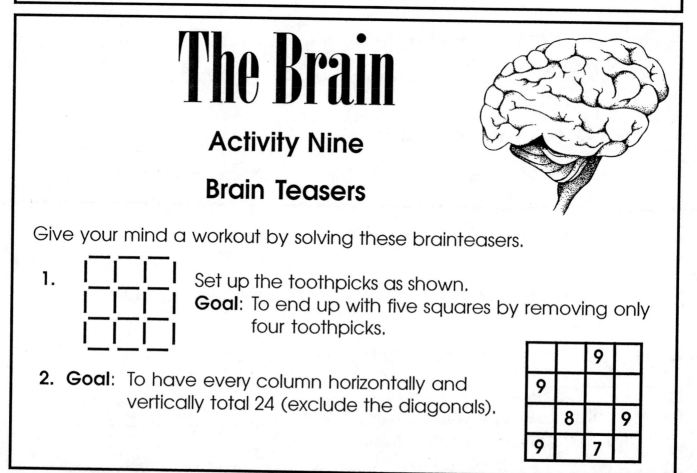

1.   Set up the toothpicks as shown.
     Goal: To end up with five squares by removing only four toothpicks.

2. **Goal:** To have every column horizontally and vertically total 24 (exclude the diagonals).

The Brain

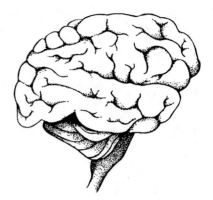

Activity Ten

Good "Sense" Writing

Good writers use their senses when they write.

Tune in to your senses as you explore the following areas to write about.

1. Using your sense of sight, write a paragraph describing a scene or an event.

    Tell about color, shape, size – everything that will help the reader **see** exactly what you see.

2. A good writer tries to make the reader **hear** a story as well as see it.

    Choose a topic to write about, paying special attention to sounds as you write.

3. You can make your writing more interesting by appealing to your reader's sense of **smell**.

    Write a paragraph describing a place, perhaps a bakery or a flower shop, paying special attention to smells. Some words that you might use are "fragrant", "spicy", "fruity", "flowery", "piny", etc.

4. Life would be quite dull without a sense of **taste**.

    Write a paragraph telling how your favorite meal tastes.

    Use words like "hot", "salty", "sweet", "sour", "tangy", "bitter", "spicy", etc.

5. The sense of **touch** is a way of learning about the things around you.

    Use touch words such as "smooth", "sleek", "rough", "sharp", "cold", "wet", etc., and write a paragraph about an animal.

    Describe it carefully, especially how it feels to the touch.

The Circulatory System

Activity One

The Heart - The Living Pump

The Circulatory System is made up of the heart, the blood vessels, and the blood. This system has a special job to do.

Read about the heart in an encyclopedia before you begin.

To understand how this system works, read the following paragraph and fill in the missing words.

Choose from the words in the box below.

aorta	auricle	bluish	carbon dioxide
chambers	cycle	red	ventricle
oxygen	vessel		

A wall of muscle separates the heart into two parts called

_____. Both chambers work at the same time and act like

pumps. Each chamber has an upper part called the _____ and

a lower part called the _____. The right pump sends oxygen-

poor and carbon dioxide-rich blood to the lungs.

In the lungs, the blood gets rid of the _____ and takes

on a fresh supply of _____. The blood with carbon dioxide is

_____ in color and the blood with oxygen is bright _____.

The left pump receives the bright red blood from the lungs and sends it to

all parts of the body through the main blood _____ called the

_____. This completes the pumping _____.

The Circulatory System

Activity Two

The Heartfelt Journey

More than one thousand times a day our blood makes a round trip through our bodies. To better understand the path of the blood as it passes through the heart, read the following directions outlined below (a red and blue colored pencil will be essential).

A) Use a blue colored pencil to represent oxygen-poor blood. Begin at the X and following the arrows, color the blood flowing into the right auricle. Continue coloring down into the right ventricle. Then follow the arrows to the lungs.

B) Use a red colored pencil to represent oxygen-rich blood. Color from the lungs, through the left auricle. Color down into the left ventricle. Follow the arrows that lead to the rest of the body.

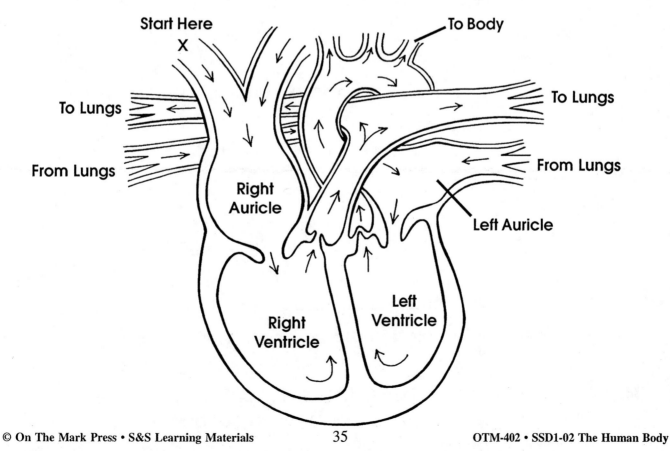

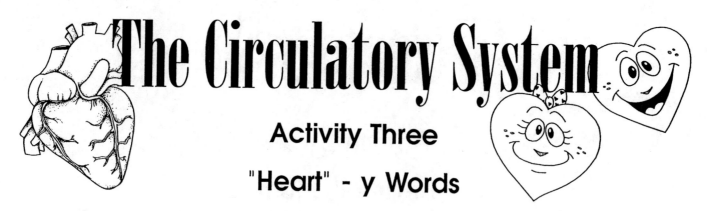

The Circulatory System

Activity Three

"Heart" - y Words

There are many words that contain the word "heart". Use the words located in the box to complete the following sentences.

hearty	hearth	heartless	heartbeat
heartfelt	heartily	heart-shaped	heartworm
heartsick	heartburn	heartbroken	heartstrings

1. The hungry boy _____ ate the whole pepperoni pizza.

2. She gave her _____ promise to her mother that she would keep her room tidy.

3. John gave a _____ laugh after hearing the joke.

4. The brick layer laid the _____ of the fireplace.

5. He suffered from _____ after eating too much cake at the birthday party.

6. Mary was _____ when she found out her dog had died.

7. The coach lost the respect of the players because he seemed cruel and _____ when he spoke to them about losing the game.

8. Michael bought his mother a _____ box of chocolates for Valentine's Day.

9. The mother was _____ when her son died in a car accident.

10. The doctor listened for my _____ with his stethoscope.

11. We gave our dog pills to protect him from getting the _____ disease.

12. The sight of the sad little puppy curled up in the corner of the cage pulled at the _____ of my heart, so I bought him.

The Circulatory System

Activity Four

"Heart" - y Pioneers

Research some scientists who have made important contributions to the study of the heart.

Write a sentence or two telling what they have discovered. Then choose one of them. Design a postage stamp to honor the scientist that you chose.

Some pioneers in the field of heart research are:

1. Dr. William Harvey
2. Dr. René Lãennec
3. Dr. Willem Einthoven

4. Dr. F. John Lewis
5. Dr. Christiaan Barnard
6. Dr. Robert Jarvik

The Circulatory System

Activity Five

Take Heart

The three best ways to take care of the heart are:

1. Exercise
2. Get plenty of rest
3. Eat the proper foods

Draw a poster showing how each of the facts is important in order to have a healthy heart.

The Circulatory System

Activity Six

Words From the Heart

Put the following "hearty" vocabulary in alphabetical order.

Then locate each word in your dictionary and write its meaning.

1. heartsick
2. heartfelt
3. heartache
4. heartland
5. heartstrings

6. hearty
7. heartbeat
8. heartless
9. heartbroken
10. heartburn

The Circulatory System

Activity Seven

Heart Art

Choose any bird, fish, or animal that interests you.

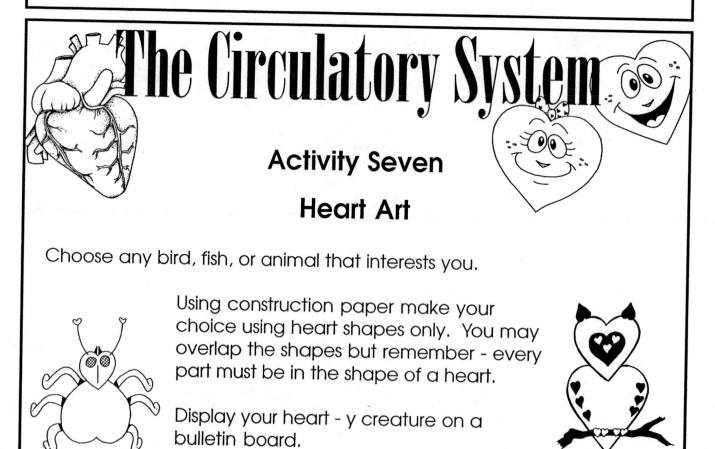

Using construction paper make your choice using heart shapes only. You may overlap the shapes but remember - every part must be in the shape of a heart.

Display your heart - y creature on a bulletin board.

The Circulatory System

Activity Eight

Exercise Word Search

One way for you to stay healthy is to exercise regularly. There are many different games and exercises to help you stay fit.

Circle those that you can find hidden in this word search. Words will be spelled up, down, backwards, or diagonally.

```
A  L  J  Q  Z  D  N  K  U  X  F  K  I  C  K  B  A  L  L  K
U  P  Z  H  N  C  Y  T  M  C  F  S  I  C  D  S  U  I  C  F
X  S  U  M  K  S  Q  M  H  F  V  J  D  A  T  C  L  F  A  V
P  R  X  C  S  H  O  N  P  R  U  N  W  F  M  H  H  R  W  Y
B  D  G  I  W  O  Y  C  F  I  W  Z  G  M  J  A  I  T  W  R
T  X  O  G  S  M  F  H  C  W  P  Z  G  A  J  S  D  A  W  R
E  G  L  A  K  L  Q  T  W  E  L  B  G  Z  Q  E  E  G  B  W
N  J  F  G  I  X  W  H  B  B  R  G  Z  S  W  J  A  L  I  G
N  Y  V  L  I  I  G  Y  T  A  R  I  G  K  B  V  N  P  C  M
I  G  X  S  N  M  M  H  B  A  A  L  F  D  A  F  K  D  K  Y  J
S  K  K  N  G  L  N  P  Q  Q  U  L  T  T  Z  Y  S  C  C  O
F  L  G  Y  M  N  A  S  T  I  C  S  S  I  Y  F  E  B  L  G
K  Q  V  F  I  S  V  X  F  K  M  V  X  N  F  M  E  O  I  G
K  V  E  C  H  V  S  W  Y  G  A  L  V  G  Q  C  K  W  N  I
L  V  S  J  G  P  V  A  J  E  P  V  J  L  G  Y  D  L  G  N
V  J  L  A  V  I  G  L  B  X  W  O  E  B  X  U  A  I  S  G
M  G  B  W  Q  O  I  K  B  Y  R  S  Q  T  Z  A  N  N  G  J
T  Z  E  J  U  M  P  R  O  P  E  J  W  P  Z  G  C  G  J  L
P  U  J  O  T  S  Y  D  B  I  T  Q  D  I  B  O  E  S  X  B
M  U  X  E  O  F  O  O  T  B  A  L  L  H  M  T  K  A  D  Y
```

football	skating	soccer	dance	kickball
chase	swim	golf	gymnastics	bowling
walk	tag	softball	jump rope	tennis
jogging	hide and seek	run	bicycling	skiing

The Circulatory System

Activity Nine

Expressions of the Heart

People use the word "heart" in many different sayings.

Some of these sayings are in **Column A**. In **Column B** are the meanings. Can you match them correctly? Record the numeral beside each saying on the line beside its meaning.

Column A

1. heart and soul
2. it does my heart good
3. his heart is in the right place
4. heartbreak
5. wear one's heart upon one's sleeve
6. his heart is in his mouth
7. eat one's heart out
8. cry your heart out
9. take things to heart
10. learn by heart
11. after my own heart
12. break my heart
13. cross my heart
14. get to the heart of
15. with all my heart and soul

Column B

____ he means well
____ lack proper reserve
____ with all one's energy
____ alarmed, startled
____ overwhelming distress
____ it makes me rejoices
____ from memory
____ pine away from anger
____ cry violently
____ to be affected by things
____ with all my love and energy
____ pleases me perfectly
____ make the sign of the cross over my heart
____ find out the secret or hidden secret
____ to make someone sad

Now try illustrating one of these sayings in its literal sense. For example "cold-hearted" could look like this:

"cold-hearted"

The Muscular System

Activity One

Muscles - Your Body's Movers

Look up the words **voluntary** and **involuntary**.

Do some research and find out what voluntary muscles and involuntary muscles are.

Why are voluntary muscles sometimes called "striped muscles"?

Can you find another name for involuntary muscles?

All of your muscles work together to produce action.

Draw an action picture of yourself playing your favorite game or sport.

The Muscular System

Activity Two

Muscles Versus Bones

Pretend that your muscles and bones are able to talk.

Each system thinks that it has a more important job to do than the other one in the movement of the body.

Divide a 23 cm X 28 cm (9" X 11") piece of drawing paper into six sections and draw a cartoon strip to illustrate the conversation between your muscles and your bones.

Be creative in your drawings.

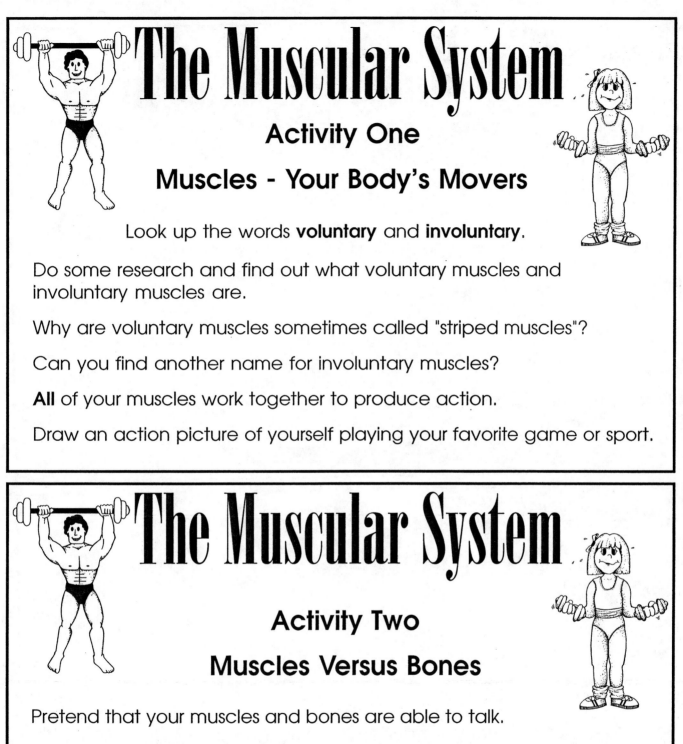

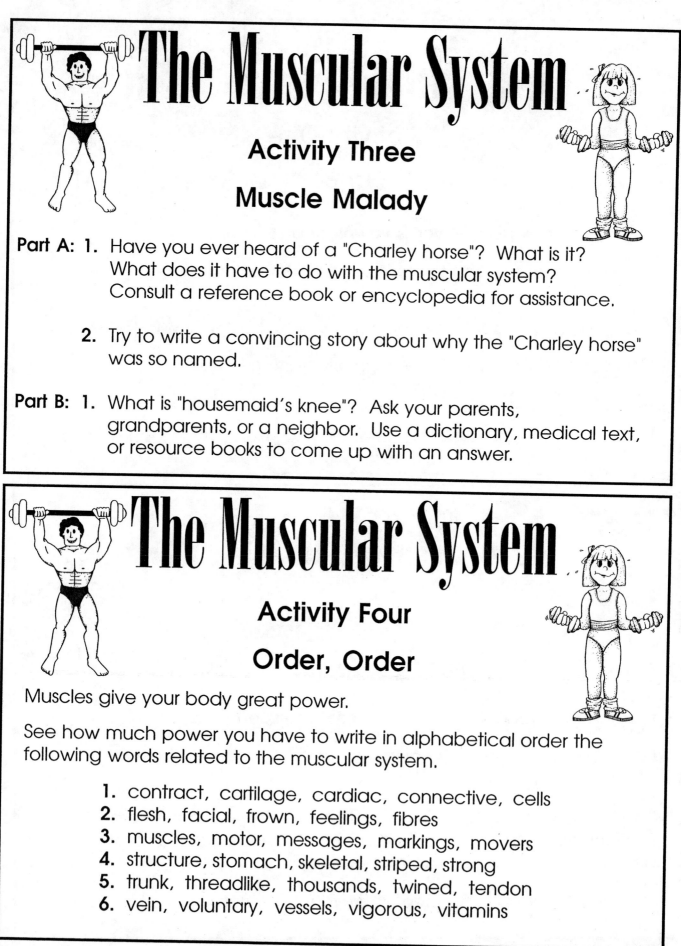

The Muscular System

Activity Three

Muscle Malady

Part A: 1. Have you ever heard of a "Charley horse"? What is it?
What does it have to do with the muscular system?
Consult a reference book or encyclopedia for assistance.

2. Try to write a convincing story about why the "Charley horse"
was so named.

Part B: 1. What is "housemaid's knee"? Ask your parents,
grandparents, or a neighbor. Use a dictionary, medical text,
or resource books to come up with an answer.

The Muscular System

Activity Four

Order, Order

Muscles give your body great power.

See how much power you have to write in alphabetical order the
following words related to the muscular system.

1. contract, cartilage, cardiac, connective, cells
2. flesh, facial, frown, feelings, fibres
3. muscles, motor, messages, markings, movers
4. structure, stomach, skeletal, striped, strong
5. trunk, threadlike, thousands, twined, tendon
6. vein, voluntary, vessels, vigorous, vitamins

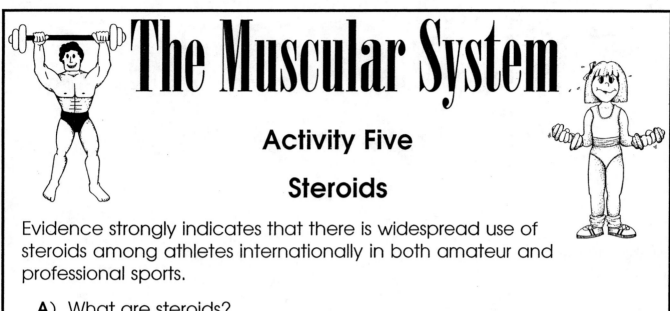

The Muscular System

Activity Five

Steroids

Evidence strongly indicates that there is widespread use of steroids among athletes internationally in both amateur and professional sports.

A) What are steroids?
How do they affect your muscles?
Why has the International Olympic Committee banned their use among participating athletes?

B) Create a poster discouraging healthy, strong athletes from using steroids.

The Muscular System

Activity Six

Let's Face It

Did you know that 17 muscles come into action when you smile and 43 muscles are needed for a frown? Save muscle power: Smile!

We communicate more easily because of these muscles. Some emotions that we can express are happiness, sadness, anger, surprise, boredom, discouragements and fear.

Choose any **two** emotions and draw a picture of a face illustrating these emotions. Pay careful attention to lines around the eyes and mouth.

Next write a short story explaining why the person in your drawing is feeling that way.

The Muscular System

Activity Seven

The Hulk

Advertising encourages people to buy certain products, especially if these products will help make someone look better or be more popular.

For example, if a world famous weight lifter did a television commercial promoting the latest in health care – "Nutri-Bulk" – sales would likely soar!

"Be like the Hulk. Take Nutri - Bulk!"

Now make up your own commercial about one of the health products listed below.

Famous people are often used to sell products.

Who would you hire to do your advertisement? Tell why.

What slogan would you use?

1. Vita-Bites (*cereal*)
2. Chocolate Nutri-Shake (*beverage*)
3. Insta-Salad (*vegetable*)
4. Fruit Chewies (*snack*)

Challenge your "brain muscle" and come up with an advertising technique that will appeal to the strong and mighty!

The Muscular System

Activity Eight

Getting the "Gist" of It

"Myologists" are people who specialize in the study of muscles.

Words that end in "- ologist" refer to people who study one particular subject.

Listed below in **Column A** are people who specialize in studying certain aspects of the human body. **Column B** lists the field in which they are specialists. Using a good dictionary or reference books, match the people in Column A with what they study in Column B.

Column A	Column B
1. myologist	___ studies the skin and hair
2. ophthalmologist	___ studies the eye
3. neurologist	___ studies bones
4. osteologist	___ studies tissues of the body
5. gastroenterologist	___ studies the kidneys
6. pathologist	___ studies the stomach
7. urologist	___ studies nerves and the brain
8. otolaryngologist	___ studies the heart
9. dermatologist	___ studies the ears, throat, and nose
10. cardiologist	___ studies muscles

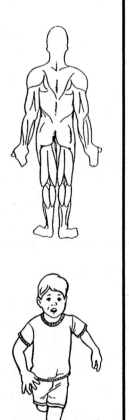

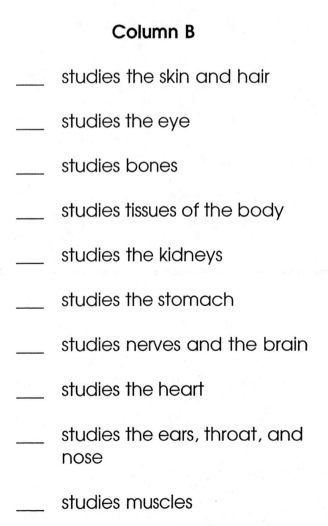

The Teeth

Activity One

The Inside Story on Teeth

In order to learn more about teeth, read the following sentences and fill in the missing words which you will find located in the box below.

bicuspids	brush	cavities	cuspids	decay
dentist	enamel	floss	incisors	molars
plaque	twelve			

1. The hard outer covering of the crown is called _____ which is the only part of the tooth visible to the eye.

2. The eight front teeth which cut food are called the _____.

3. Four teeth called _____ tear up food into smaller bits. These teeth have a point.

4. When you get your permanent set of teeth, you get eight _____ which are used to crush your food into smaller pieces. These teeth have two points.

5. The real work of chewing is done with the _____ in the back of your mouth. You will have _____ of these when all your permanent teeth come in.

6. The most common problem with teeth among children is tooth _____. This begins in the enamel and spreads into the dentine.

7. _____ is the sticky layer of harmful bacteria that is constantly forming on your teeth.

8. Foods containing sugar encourage tooth decay. In the presence of sweets, bacteria form acids. These acids cause _____.

9. It is wise to _____ and _____ after eating.

10. To help prevent tooth decay visit your _____ regularly.

The Teeth

Activity Two

The Whole Tooth

Using the following terms, label the teeth in the diagrams below.

Use a resource book for assistance if necessary.

cuspids, incisors, molars, enamel, crown, pulp, root, dentine

Some words may be used more than once.

Parts of a Tooth

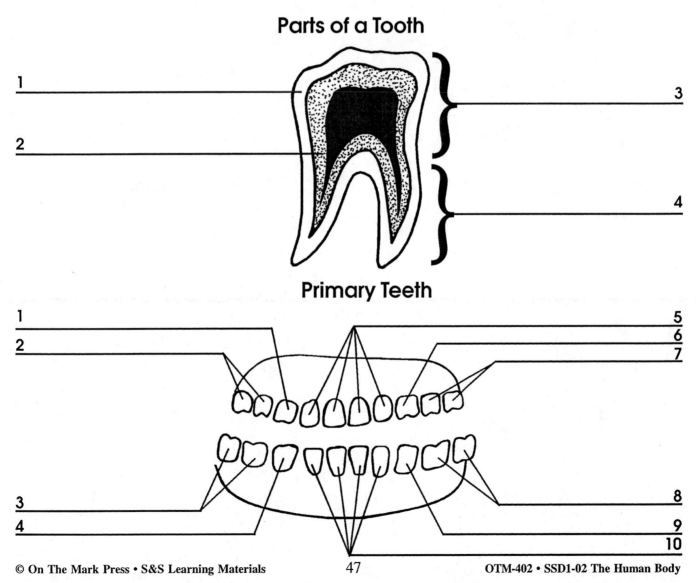

Primary Teeth

The Teeth

Activity Three

Dental Health Quiz

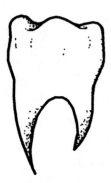

Think up six quiz questions pertaining to Dental Health.

Begin each question using a different word – **who, what, where, why, when**, and **how**.

For guidance and inspiration consult encyclopedias, health books, and other available resource materials.

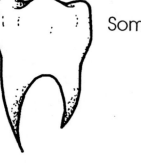

Some examples are:

1. **How** do the gums act to protect your teeth?

2. **Who** has stronger teeth – a child or a dog?

3. **Which** machine determines whether you have cavities or not?

Be sure to answer your six questions on lined paper. Try your quiz on a classmate.

If everyone participates in this activity, the students may write out their questions and put them into a "Dental Health Quiz Box".

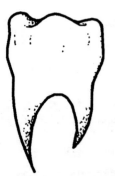

Teams may be selected and members may take turns quizzing their opponents.

After an allotted time span, the team having the most members still participating would win.

The Teeth

Activity Four

My Wobbly Tooth

I bit into my apple
And what happened, do you think?
My wobbly tooth
Came out as fast as a wink!
I'll put it under my pillow tonight.
I wonder if the tooth fairy will come
When I turn out the light?

Try your own hand at writing a poem about teeth.

The Teeth

Activity Five

Toothy Alliteration

See how good you are at composing a tongue twister about dental health.

Try it on a classmate.

Here are two to get you started.

1. *Clean cuspids cut cucumbers crisply.*

2. *Magnificent molars make miraculous mighty munchers.*

The Teeth

Activity Six

Brush Up on Toothbrushes!

Do some research and find out how the practice of brushing teeth began.

Write a paragraph about your findings.

Draw a picture of what you think the **first** toothbrush looked like.

Draw a humorous situation illustrating the use of early toothbrushes.

The Teeth

Activity Seven

Toothbrush to the Rescue

Create a super hero whose secret weapon is a toothbrush!

What will you call him?
What will he wear?
Whom will he protect?
What does he look like?

Draw a picture of your super hero and write a story about one of his adventures.

Be creative! Have fun!

The Teeth

Activity Eight

The Tooth Fairy

Losing that first tooth is such an exhilarating feeling!

You are so anxious to get that tiny, pearly-white tooth to drop into your hand.

You twisted, pulled, yanked, and fiddled until at last you had that precious possession to put under your pillow that night.

The "tooth fairy" would come and leave some shiny coins and take your tooth. It was a miraculous and magical event.

Let your imagination wander to the land of the tooth fairies.

What is their fairyland like and how does it look?
How many fairies live there?
What do they look like?
Do they watch over children and wait for that special moment?
Where do the tooth fairies get all that money that they leave?
Do they have a secret cavern overflowing with gold and silver?

Create a story about this mystical land of the tooth fairies. Write it as a storybook for younger children.

Describe what you would see, hear, and feel in "The Land of the Tooth Fairy". Tell about the joy, the peace, the love and the beauty that surrounds this land.

Add colorful illustrations as well.

The Teeth

Activity Nine
Plaque Attack

A jingle is a short rhyme.

Think of a good jingle for dental health care.

Write it out and then record it on a tape recorder.

Perhaps you could even broadcast your jingle on the school's P.A. system during Dental Health Month.

Example:
*Teeth, teeth
Be sure to keep them clean,
So all thirty-two can proudly be seen.
Brush them, floss them, front and back.
Be prepared for plaque attack!*

The Teeth

Activity Ten

Say Cheese!

Make a picture collage of smiles.

Cut pictures from magazines showing teeth and glue them onto a piece of manilla paper.

Try to find a variety of pictures showing healthy teeth, a missing tooth, teeth with braces, etc.

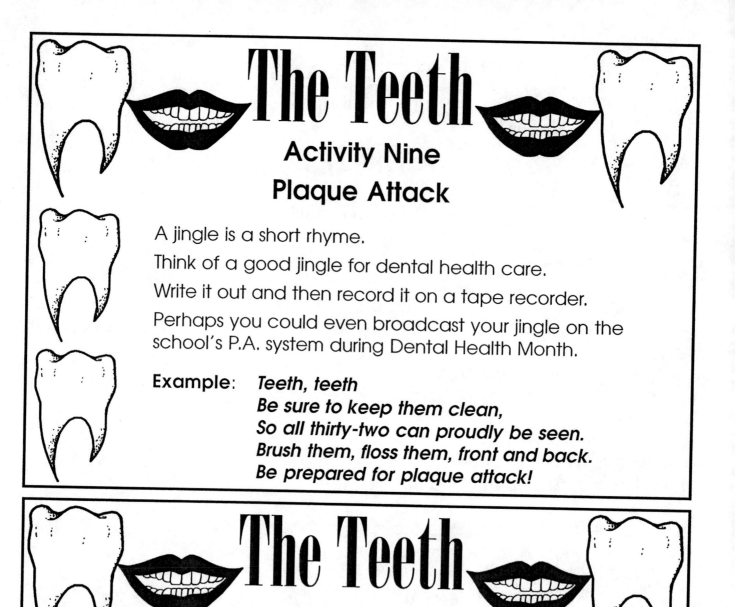

The Teeth

Activity Eleven

Story Starters

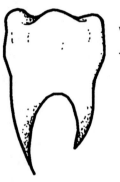

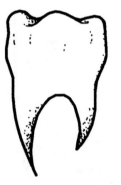

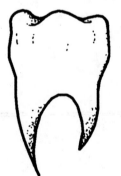

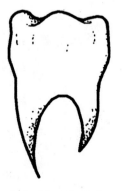

Write an interesting story about teeth by using one of the following ideas.

1. A trip to the dentist results in you receiving radio transmissions through your new filling!

2. All your teeth started to shudder when they saw a large chocolate bunny approaching them.

3. A very interesting thing happened to you when you were on your way to the dentist.

4. This morning, you looked in the mirror and smiled. You were about to brush your teeth but you suddenly saw something strange.

5. The photographer was about to take your picture. He said, "Say cheese". You did, and he dropped his camera.

6. The other night you were watching television and eating your favorite junk food when suddenly......

7. When I was six years old I discovered my front tooth was loose. I kept wiggling it but it would not come out. So my father.........

8. I can remember the day I had such a terrible toothache. I was in such...........

9. One day I played a trick on my grandfather. I took his false teeth out of the glass where they were soaking. I decided to.........

The Teeth

Activity Twelve

A Visit to the Dentist

Write a poem or a story, accompanied by a drawing, to tell what happens when a "zoo dentist" treats animals at the zoo.

What would this dentist use for tools - perhaps a hammer or a screwdriver or a large pair of forceps?

How would he get the animal to open his mouth?

Would a walrus have a toothache or a "tusk" ache?

Be creative!

The Teeth

Activity Thirteen

Safety Rules

Think of the most common causes of accidents to teeth.

Create a list of safety rules which could be followed by you and your classmates in school and on the playground.

Display the list in your classroom.

Try to think of **ten** good safety rules that could prevent accidents that break or chip teeth.

Here are two to get you started.
1. Do not push at water fountains.
2. Do not throw stones.

The Respiratory System

Activity One

How We Breathe

Use the words in the box below to complete the sentences about the respiratory system.

alveoli	breathing	bronchial	bronchioles	bronchus	cells
contraction	diaphragm	exhalation		heart	inhalation
lungs	larynx	nose	oxygen	pharynx	trachea
trunk	carbon dioxide				

The respiratory organs consist of the _____, _____ (throat), _____ (voice box), _____ (windpipe), the _____ tubes and the _____. Together they form the respiratory system, which supplies the body with _____ and removes waste _____.

Air is moved in and out of the respiratory system by _____. During _____ (breathing in), air is drawn in through the nose, pharynx, trachea and bronchi and into the lungs. Inside the lungs, each _____ divides repeatedly to form what looks like an upside-down tree. The trachea is like the _____ of the tree. It branches into two main bronchi, which branch into _____. The smallest bronchioles end in clusters of tiny airbags called _____. Oxygen from the air that reaches the alveoli passes into the blood capillaries. This oxygen-rich blood is first carried to the _____ and is then pumped to _____ throughout the body. Carbon dioxide passes from the blood into the alveoli and is removed from the body during _____ (breathing out).

Breathing is the result of muscular _____. During inhalation, the _____ (a dome-shaped muscle that lies beneath the lungs) tenses and flattens. Muscles between the ribs pull the ribs upward and outwards. The chest stretches and air is drawn into the lungs. When you breathe out, the chest springs back and air flows out.

The Respiratory System

Activity Two

Labeling a Diagram

Use the words listed in the box below to label the diagram of the respiratory system.

alveoli	diaphragm	mouth cavity
bronchi	larynx	nasal cavity
bronchial tube	lobes of lung	pharynx
trachea		

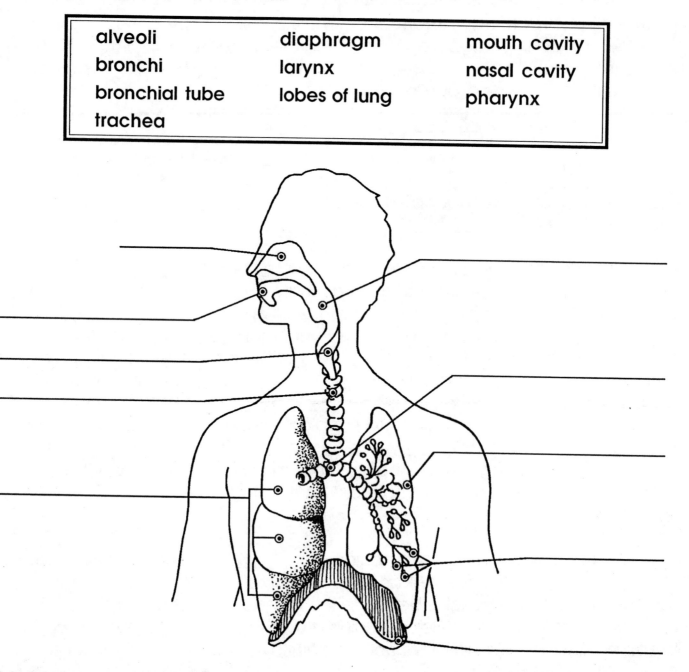

The Respiratory System

Activity Three

Respiratory Scramble

The following parts of the respiratory system have been scrambled.
Try to unscramble them using the clues to help identify the terms.

1. **A T N O B R U C H B E I L** _____

   (*either of the two main branches leading into the lungs*)

2. **O E N S** _____

   (*facial feature where air is taken in*)

3. **A R T H A C E** _____

   (*the windpipe; passage by which air is carried from the throat to the lungs*)

4. **L I O N O R B C H E** _____

   (*small air tubes that end in alveoli*)

5. **A P D A M G H I R** _____

   (*a partition of muscles and tendons separating the chest cavity from
   the abdominal cavity*)

6. **S N L G U** _____

   (*organs that oxygenate the blood and remove carbon dioxide from it*)

7. **L I V O E L A** _____

   (*the air pockets in the lungs*)

8. **S T O G P I L I T E** _____

   (*a thin plate of cartilage that prevents tfood from entering the lungs*)

9. **Y A R H X N P** _____

   (*the throat; air is drawn in through the nose and throat during inhalation*)

10. **A R Y N L X** _____

    (*the voice box which links the pharynx with the trachea*)

The Respiratory System

Activity Four

Catch Your Breath

Read the following information about respiratory diseases. Then take the time to "catch your breath, and begin the following activities.

The respiratory system is the system of the body that deals with breathing. Consequently, respiratory diseases affect those parts of the body that are utilized to enable us to breathe. One of the most frequent things that affects our respiratory system is the common cold which is usually caused by a virus. Drinking lots of fluids, especially water, is helpful, but when symptoms persist, it is important to consult a doctor.

Bronchitis can develop from a constant cold. However, it can also be the result of lung infections, measles, heart disease, other infections, or smoking. Treatment varies and may include medication to loosen the phlegm or to fight the infection. Humidifiers used at night help a person to breathe while sleeping.

Respiratory allergies can be anything from year-round nasal allergies to hay fever or asthma. Symptoms from these allergies are treated or relieved by drugs.

Another disease is called emphysema. This disease cannot be cured by drugs. Lung surgery can be helpful to the patient. Smoking, air pollution, and genetics are factors in contracting this disease.

Bacteria causes a disease known as tuberculosis. Today this disease is controlled in many countries by a vaccine called BCG. If tuberculosis is contacted by a person there are several drugs used to cure this disease.

Lung cancer is mainly caused by smoking. It is a major killer in our society. Chemotherapy and the use of drugs are the best treatments but success is found only with early diagnosis.

The Respiratory System

Activity Four

Catch Your Breath

A) Use the vocabulary found in the box below to complete the sentences that pertain to respiratory diseases.

common cold	allergy	bronchitis	humidifier	pneumonia
tuberculosis	phlegm	asthma	virus	emphysema

1. The most widespread of all diseases is the _____.

2. A body reaction which occurs in a person who is sensitive to certain substances is an _____.

3. A thick mucus which is present in many respiratory diseases is called _____.

4. A very serious infectious disease which can be diagnosed with a skin test but may take a very long time to cure is _____.

5. Many cases of _____ start as chronic bronchitis.

6. Partial blocking of the bronchial tubes brings on attacks of _____.

7. Inflammation of the bronchial tubes is called _____.

8. _____ results as a complication of colds and bronchitis.

9. A _____ is a machine that moisturizes the air to help improve breathing.

10. A cold is usually caused by a _____.

The Respiratory System

Activity Four

Catch Your Breath

B) The best advice on cigarette smoking is still that given by the American Heart Association: "Be Smart, Don't Start".

The lungs are made up of five hundred million air sacs. Microscopic slides of diseased lungs often show large deposits of carbon on the lungs and this condition is known as "black lung". Smoking can lead to this problem and it often develops into cancer.

Brainstorm poster ideas that will help increase the awareness of the dangers of smoking among your peers. The examples below may help you to get started.

The Respiratory System

Activity Five

Voyage to the Lungs

Like a journey the respiratory system is an ongoing trip. Embark on your "Voyage to the Lungs" by filling in the blanks using the word bank provided.

trachea	nose	bronchi	alveoli
cilia	throat	mouth	larynx
diaphragm	lungs		

1. Air enters our respiratory system through the _____ and _____.

2. Dust and other dirt particles are prevented from reaching the _____ by tiny hairs called _____.

3. When we inhale, the _____, which is a large muscle, assists our lungs to expand in order to take in air.

4. Air then passes through the _____ to the voice box or _____.

5. From here it moves through the windpipe which is also known as the _____.

6. Next, the _____, which are two tubes, carry the air to the lungs.

7. The air finally reaches millions of _____ which take the oxygen to the blood.

The Respiratory System

Activity Six

In and Out

Study the two charts then answer these questions.

1. Which has more carbon dioxide, inhaled or exhaled air?

   _____
   _____
   _____
   _____

2. Does the amount of nitrogen in inhaled and exhaled air differ?

   _____
   _____
   _____
   _____

3. How much of the oxygen inhaled remains in the body?

   _____
   _____
   _____
   _____

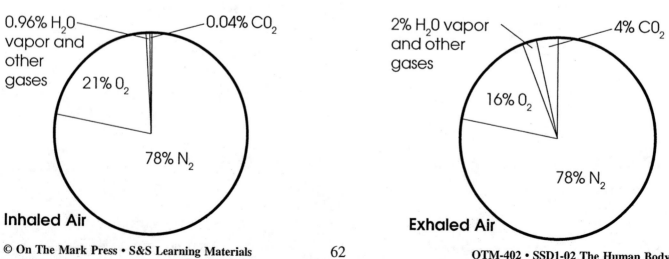

0.96% H_2O vapor and other gases — 0.04% CO_2 — 21% O_2 — 78% N_2

Inhaled Air

2% H_2O vapor and other gases — 4% CO_2 — 16% O_2 — 78% N_2

Exhaled Air

The Digestive System

Activity One

How Our Food is Digested

Use the words in the word bank to complete the information that describes the way food is digested in your body.

liquid	digestion	gastrointestinal	saliva	rectum
liver	undigested	gall bladder	chyme	gastric
calories	alimentary	peristalsis	bile	large
waste	bloodstream	solid	muscles	stomach
intestine	esophagus	pancreas		

Food is the fuel that provides energy for your body. The energy is measured in units called _____. Before your body can use the food you eat, it has to be broken down into tiny bits that are small enough to pass into your blood. This _____ takes approximately twenty hours as the food travels through a long tube that is located between the mouth and the rectum. This system is also known as the _____ tract or the _____ tract.

The digestive system is made up of several organs which are each responsible for a specific task when digesting food.

The digestion process begins as you take your first bite of food. The spit or _____ in your mouth has a digestive juice that starts to break down the food. It then travels down a foodpipe called the _____. Food is pushed along inside this foodpipe by rings of _____. The pushing and squeezing action of the muscles is called _____. Food then enters the _____ where it is mixed with _____ juices. Food is partly digested in the stomach.

The Digestive System

Activity One

How Our Food is Digested (continued)

Then the food material moves into the small _____. It is in the form of a thick liquid called _____. Chyme is squeezed out of the stomach into the small intestine a little at a time. The small intestine is a coiled tube which, if straightened, would be about four times your height! Digestive juices come from the small intestine's walls and are mixed with food by the movements of the small intestine. Other digestive juices are made by the _____ and the _____. Juice made by the liver, called _____ or gall, is stored in the _____. Digestion of food is completed in the small intestine. Most of the food by this time has changed into a thin, watery form that passes out of the small intestine and goes into the _____. Some food cannot be digested, or broken down in the small intestine.

The _____ food is pushed by muscles into the _____ intestine where it gradually becomes _____ material which is eventually pushed out of the body through the _____. While the large intestine gets rid of the _____ wastes, the kidneys help get rid of _____ wastes.

The Digestive System

Activity Two

Labeling a Diagram

Use the parts listed in the box below to label the drawing of the human digestive system.

large intestine	salivary glands	stomach	small intestine
esophagus	pancreas	liver	tongue
rectum			

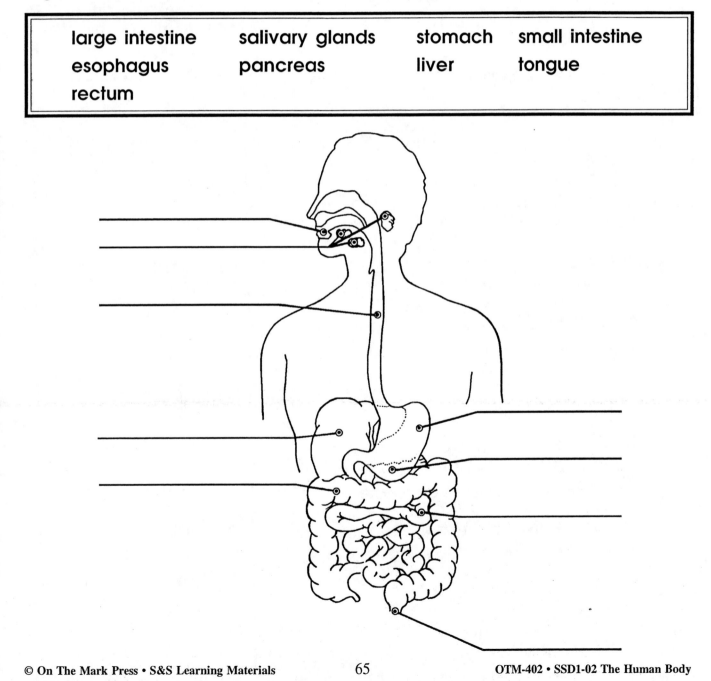

The Digestive System

Activity Three

Can You Stomach This?

When we think about digestion the one body organ that comes to mind is the stomach. However, the digestive system involves numerous body organs and the process is quite complex. Recall the facts you have learned so far and see if you have the "stomach" to successfully complete the following activity.

Place the letter of the correct answer next to the definition.

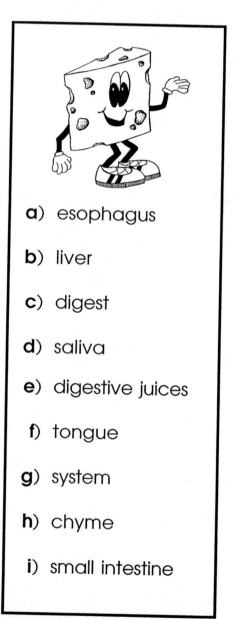

_____ 1. makes dry food wet and hard food soft

_____ 2. turns food and pushes it between your teeth

_____ 3. food and juices mix together several hours to form this liquid

_____ 4. a long tube from the mouth to the stomach

_____ 5. to change food to a substance the body can use

_____ 6. after leaving the stomach, chyme enters this part of the body where it is broken down even further

_____ 7. juices from this organ enter the small intestine to break down food

_____ 8. a group of body parts

_____ 9. these soak into the walls of the small intestine

a) esophagus

b) liver

c) digest

d) saliva

e) digestive juices

f) tongue

g) system

h) chyme

i) small intestine

The Digestive System

Activity Four

Word Search

Hidden in the grid are eight digestive organs. They may be found vertically, horizontally, or diagonally.

Circle the following words as you find them:

pharynx	mouth	small intestine
stomach	liver	large intestine
esophagus	pancreas	

```
P A N C V E S T O M A L I V P
M A N C H X Y S T P H A G U A
S B L L F A B U M P L E R S N
T O P I L P A C R O L F E R C
O V H E V X N E S T U N L P R
M L A R G E I N T E S T I N E
A V R E S T R O Z L C D H U A
C S Y B M A L I N T E S N E S
H I N E S O P H A G U S E R C
L I X N M Q S U W Y P H I M N
O P R T V X Z M R N R T W Y A
S M A L L I N T E S T I N E P
```

On a separate piece of paper write the words and tell how each of the organs helps in the digestion of food.

The Digestive System

Activity Five

Facts to Digest

Digestion is the breakdown of food into simple compounds that can be used by the body. The digestive system prepares the food so the cells can use it, absorbs the food into the body, and eliminates waste material which cannot be absorbed. There are many interesting "facts to digest" regarding this system of our body.

For example, we've all heard either our own or someone else's stomach "growl". What causes this? Actually, it happens when the stomach wall squeezes together to mix and digest the food but there is no food. So, consequently, gases and digestive juices churn around in the empty stomach and make a noise which doctors call "borborygmi"! Quite a name for something so common, isn't it?

A) Below are some other intriguing "facts to digest". Read them carefully, then rewrite the facts putting in all the necessary capitals and punctuation marks.

1. your digestive tract is approximately 9.25 meters (30.35 feet) long

   _____

   _____

   _____

2. carbohydrates fats and protein are a good source of energy fats can give us the most energy fifteen milliliters ($\frac{1}{2}$ oz) of fat yields about one hundred calories

   _____

   _____

   _____

3. a person who weighs approximately 45.4 kilograms (100 lb) uses 200 calories per hour for active playing and 50 calories per hour to sleep

   _____

   _____

   _____

The Digestive System

Facts to Digest (continued)

4. dr. william beaumont put juice from a patients stomach in a bottle and dropped in a piece of meat this took about ten hours to digest

_____

_____

_____

5. throughout the digestive process food remains in the stomach for as long as approximately six hours

_____

_____

_____

6. plant fibers in a person's diet can help prevent the development of cancer of the digestive tract

_____

_____

_____

7. a normal active fifteen year old male needs an average of 3 000 calories per day on the other hand a normal active fifteen year old female needs only 2 500 calories per day

_____

_____

_____

B) It is also a fact that the digestion of food supplies body cells with materials for energy, repair, and growth. This process is quite complex and involves a long step-by-step process. Using a dictionary and/or other resource materials write a sentence or two telling how each of the following words relate to the digestive system.

1. enzymes: _____

_____

_____

The Digestive System

Facts to Digest (continued)

2. chyme: _____

_____

_____

3. peristalsis: _____

_____

_____

4. bile: _____

_____

_____

5. bolus: _____

_____

_____

6. pepsin: _____

_____

_____

7. metabolize: _____

_____

_____

The Digestive System

Activity Six

Down the Hatch

How does your body use digested food material which is carried by the blood to all parts of the body?

The digested food has nourishing materials in it called **nutrients**. There are many different nutrients found in foods. **Fats** and **carbohydrates** provide you with energy. **Vitamins** and **minerals** keep you healthy. **Proteins** build cells and help your body to grow and repair itself. To be well-nourished each day, you must eat foods that contain these nutrients in the right amounts. There is no single food that contains all the nutrients in the amounts you need.

A) Do some research and find out which foods contain which nutrients. Write them under the following headings on a chart like the one below.

Fats	Carbohydrates	Vitamins	Minerals	Proteins

B) Which organs and processes do these nutrients help?

C) From old magazines, cut out pictures of foods that are good for your body. Write on the pictures the nutrients those foods contain.

Nutrition

Activity One

Nutrition Squad

Healthy eating depends on eating food each day from four food groups.

Nutritionists have divided the foods we need into these groups:

Milk and Milk Products
Fruits and Vegetables
Bread and Cereal
Meat and Fish

Choose a food from each group and make a poster advertising the importance of good eating. Dress up your foods as characters and give them a name. For example, "Captain Cereal", "Carlotta Carrot", "Frederick Fish", "Milton Milk". Perhaps you could call them the "Nutrition Squad".

Let your characters talk and write a message promoting healthy foods.

Question: What do ducks snack on?

Answer: Cheese and quackers

A Food Guide

THESE FOODS ARE GOOD TO EAT!
EAT THEM EVERY DAY FOR HEALTH!
HAVE THREE MEALS EACH DAY!

MILK

Children (up to about 11 years) ... 2 1/2 cups (20 fl. oz.)
Adolescents .... 4 cups (32 fl. oz.)
Adults .... 1 1/2 cups (12 fl.oz.)
Expectant and nursing mothers .... 4 cups (32 fl. oz.)

FRUIT

Two servings of fruit or juice including a satisfactory source of vitamin C (ascorbic acid) such as oranges, tomatoes, or vitaminized apple juice.

VEGETABLES

One serving of potatoes.
Two servings of other vegetables, preferably yellow or green and often raw.

BREAD AND CEREALS

Bread (with butter or fortified margarine).
One serving of whole grain cereal.

MEAT AND FISH

One serving of meat, fish, or poultry.
Eat liver occasionally.
Eggs, cheese, and dried beans or peas may be used in place of meat.
In addition, have eggs and cheese at least three times a week.

Nutrition

Activity Two

Nutri-Wise

Read the following situation. Then apply your nutritional knowledge to answer the questions. If necessary, first familiarize yourself with the four basic food groups and their importance to our general health.

Due to a natural disaster a small isolated village became blocked off from the rest of civilization. Roads were wiped out and it would take at least a week before relief efforts would be able to reach the survivors. Food from the local grocery store could be shared for the time being. However, before long fresh fruit and vegetables would be depleted. What would the villagers do then?

1. What may be used as a meat substitute?

2. What may be used to substitute fresh fruit and vegetables?

3. What may the villagers use instead of fresh milk?

4. When the relief effort does arrive it will only be able to bring one load of food. What do you suggest this load should consist of?

Become a real dietician – read, study, and read some more until you feel confident in answering these questions. Remember you are responsible for the lives of others, so do not include any "empty" calories in your relief package. **Be nutrition wise!**

Nutrition

Activity Three

Pumping Iron

Iron is one of the minerals our bodies require for good health. Our bodies use iron to make haemoglobin in red blood cells. Iron combines with food to produce the energy we need to move, to grow, and to heat our bodies.

Not many foods are rich in iron so it is not always easy to get the necessary iron. One food rich in iron is liver - not everyone's favorite food! Others are beans, sesame seeds, prunes, raisins, broccoli, tomato juice, sardines and whole-grain or enriched cereals.

Make an illustrated booklet of foods rich in iron. You may want to call it "Ironclad Foods".

Question: What is a parrot's favorite fish dish?

Answer: Perch

Nutrition

Activity Four

Food Trivia

Test your knowledge about various foods. Read the following statements and write a sentence or two about each, expressing your opinion. Upon completion check your responses with resource books or encyclopedias. Then tally your score as follows:

0 - 3 correct - inadequate knowledge
4 - 6 correct - average to good knowledge
7 - 10 correct - very good knowledge

Are the following statements true or false?

1. Foods high in protein such as fish contain very few calories. _____

2. There are more calories in butter than in margarine. _____

3. Potatoes are very fattening. _____

4. There are no calories in vitamins and minerals. _____

5. Leaving food in an open can in the refrigerator is a very dangerous practice. _____

6. Taking vitamin tablets is the best way to provide the necessary vitamins in your diet.

7. Fruit juices can be fattening if we drink more than we actually need. _____

8. Tomatoes can actually help the blood to clot if we have a cut. _____

9. Eating too many eggs is not good for you. _____

10. You should eat like a king at breakfast, a queen at lunch time and a pauper at dinner time. _____

Nutrition

Activity Five

Food for Thought

Think about the following problems about food and try to solve them. When you are finished, try to think of one of your own.

1. In one day John consumed 3 275 calories. However, for his size and age he should be consuming only 2 850 calories. How many calories should be cut from his diet?

2. Rewrite the following recipe using one half of all the ingredients.

Pancakes

$\frac{3}{4}$ cup of whole wheat flour

$\frac{1}{4}$ cup of wheat germ

$\frac{1}{2}$ cup of all purpose flour

1 tbsp. baking powder

2 tbsp. salt

1 egg beaten

$1\frac{1}{4}$ cups of skim milk

2 tbsp. vegetable oil

Nutrition

Food for Thought (continued)

3. The grade five class is having a chocolate chip cookie sale at school to raise money for their school trip. If the students baked 600 cookies and they were putting 5 cookies in each bag, how many bags of cookies would they have to sell? If they sold all the cookies at 25 cents per bag, how much money would the grade five class raise?

4. If we gave breakfast food values, as in the chart below, create a breakfast that would be worth 14 points, 21 points, and 3 points. What's the value of the breakfast that you ate this morning?

Breakfast Points		
Pancake - 2	Egg - 2	Syrup - 1
Butter - 1	Bread - 4	Fruit - 3
Milk - 6	Juice - 5	Yogurt - 3
Bacon - 2	Cereal - 3	All other foods - 0

5. You ordered the following foods in a restaurant:

Milkshake - $1.59
Chicken Nuggets - $2.09
French Fries - $1.09
Apple Pie - $1.49

What is the total price?
If you gave the waitress $20.00, how much change did you receive?

Nutrition

Activity Six

Sensible Snacking

Healthy snacks, rather than junk food, are important to eat between meals.

Can you think of a snack for each letter in the words "healthy snacks" that would satisfy a nutritionist?

H - hard boiled eggs

E - _____

A - _____

T - _____

H - _____

Y - _____

S - _____

N - _____

A - apple

C - _____

K - kabobs made from vegetables

S - _____

Question: What snack can you wear on your head?

Answer: A homburger

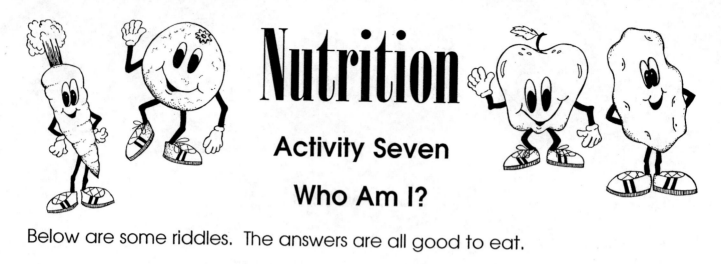

Nutrition

Activity Seven

Who Am I?

Below are some riddles. The answers are all good to eat.

Which fruit or vegetable is each riddle referring to?

1. Popeye likes to eat me. _____

2. I have an ear but it cannot hear. _____

3. I have eyes but they cannot see. _____

4. I'm okay to eat. My name starts with OK. _____

5. I have a heart but it cannot beat. _____

6. I have spears which are not sharp. _____

7. You cannot tie my strings. _____

8. I have a head but no hair. _____

9. I have great ap-peel to monkeys. _____

10. Redheads are sometimes nicknamed after me. _____

Nutrition

Activity Eight

Food Label Study

It's important to "know" what exactly is in the foods that you eat every day. Some ingredients are good for you, yet others are not.

From home, bring in seven or eight **food labels** from packages or jars such as barbecue sauce, crackers, potato chips, and so on.

Look up the ingredients in your dictionary to find out what each means. For example, dextrose in candy is made from cornstarch and the algin in ice cream comes from seaweed.

I'm sure that after completing this activity, you will be very careful about reading the labels on packaging before you eat something.

Now select several labels and make a poster listing the ingredients and what they are.

Display the finished product for your classmates to read in an interesting format.

Nutrition

Activity Nine

How Many Ways Can You Say Eat?

Try to come up with a word for every letter of the alphabet that means the same or almost the same as "eat".

Use a dictionary or a thesaurus to help you. Some words are filled in to get you started.

A - _____

B - _____

C - _____

D - _____

E - _____

F - _____

G - _____

H - _____

I - _____

J - _____

K - _____

L - lick

M - munch

N - nibble

O - _____

P - _____

Q - _____

R - _____

S - snack

T - _____

U - _____

V - _____

W - _____

X - _____

Y - _____

Z - _____

Nutrition

Activity Ten

"Dairy" Good

Read the following information about ice cream ingredients.

Then try to fill in the blanks using the words listed in the box to complete the story about ice cream.

You may need to use some resource books and a dictionary.

bananas	cane	kelp	dextrose
corn syrup	eggs	beet	locust beans
vanilla beans	pineapple	cacao beans	strawberries
Irish moss			

_____, _____ and _____ are

stabilizers. They give ice cream its smooth, creamy texture and also help

the ice cream to hold its shape. _____ are an additional

ingredient which help in stiffening the ice cream, while at the same time

enriching it. Two sugars used in ice cream are _____ and

_____ sugar. Corn sweeteners are sometimes added to help

make the ice cream firmer. Two examples of these are _____

and _____. Ice cream is flavored by using a variety of items -

_____, _____, _____ _____ and

_____.

Nutrition

Activity Eleven

What's "New" - tritional in Foods?

Fast food has become very popular these days. Today people are constantly in a hurry and they wish to eat quickly as time is a precious commodity.

Pretend that you have invented a nutritious fast food pill.

A) What color would your fast food pill be?

What kind of flavors would you make?

Would your pill last an entire meal?

What kinds of foods would you put in your fast food pills for breakfast, lunch, or dinner?

What type of snack pills would you make?

Describe the color and texture of each "new" - tritional fast food pill that you have invented.

B) Design a poster promoting your "new"- tritional food pills.

Nutrition

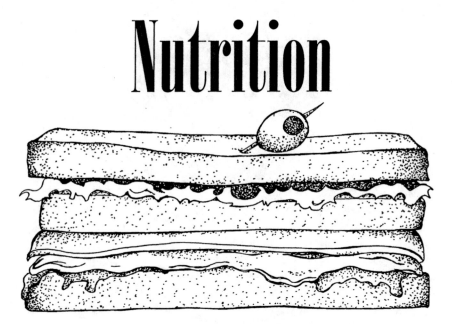

Activity Twelve

Out to Lunch

Sandwiches were named after the Earl of Sandwich, an English nobleman of the 1700s. He ordered a servant to bring him two slices of bread with a piece of roasted meat between them. It was then that the sandwich was born!

Let's amaze the Earl by inventing a super-sandwich.

Your sandwich can have any combination of ingredients as long as they are nutritious. Perhaps you will create one for vegetarians or perhaps one to eat at breakfast, or perhaps a pizza sandwich. Try a food other than bread for your holder, such as waffles, English muffins, buns, and fancy breads.

Be creative. Have fun and maybe try your creation at home.

Bon Appétit!

Nutrition

Activity Thirteen

The Cholesterol Question

Today people are generally very health conscious. Recent studies have revealed that some diseases may be prevented if one adheres to a proper, nutritionally sound diet. Such a diet would include reduced cholesterol intake. There is a greater public awareness about "cholesterol" intake these days.

1. What actually is "cholesterol"?
2. How many types are there?
3. How does "cholesterol" affect our bodies?

A) Research and write your report in several well constructed paragraphs.

B) Pretend the Department of Health is sponsoring a contest and they ask students to create a "super-hero" and "slogan" that could be used to discourage people from indulging in high cholesterol foods.

The winner will have the privilege of seeing their super-hero and slogan printed on billboards, bumper stickers, and posters nation-wide.

Do your best to promote sound nutrition!

Answer Key

The Skeletal System

"Bone" -y Terminology: *(page 8)*
1. ligaments   2. joint   3. marrow   4. jawbone   5. fracture   6. coccyx
7. tendons

"Boning Up" on Information: *(page 9)*
1. One billion (plus)   2. 206   3. calcium   4. in your hands and feet
5. 29 different bones   6. the spine   7. femur   8. elbow
9. ribs   10. marrow

Mr. Skelly-Ton - Part A: *(page 10)*
femur 3, cranium 8, tibia 9, ulna 4, sternum 10, tarsals 1, patella 2, phalanx 5,
clavicle 6, mandible 7, radius 4

Mr. Skelly-Ton - Part B: *(page 11)*
1. clavicle   2. femur   3. tarsals   4. cranium   5. mandible   6. sternum
7. radius   8. ulna   9. phalanx   10. patella   11. tibia

Skeleton Mystery: *(page 12)*
Hidden picture: A hand.

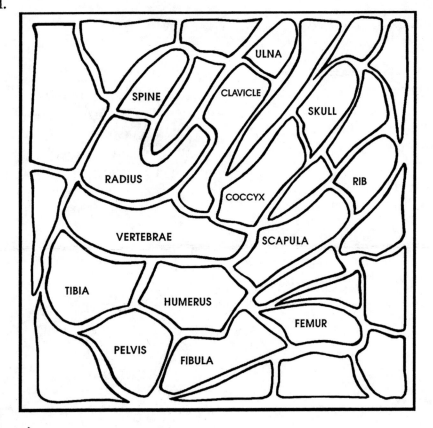

Body Sayings: *(page 13)*
1. thumb   2. knee   3. skin   4. leather   5. stomach   6. heart   7. neck
8. hair   9. ear   10. nose   11. skeleton   12. heart

Math for Every-"body": *(page 14)*
Answers may vary.

Dermotolyphics: *(page 15)*
Answers may vary.

A "Hip" -py Tune: *(page 16)*
Answers may vary.

Mr. Bones: *(page 16)*
Answers may vary.

Bone Up on Writing: *(page 17)*
Answers may vary.

Bare Bones: *(page 18)*
Answers may vary.

Bone-less: *(page 18)*
Answers may vary.

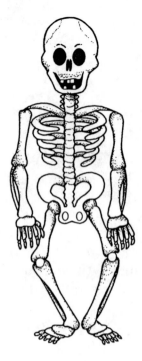

Get Off on the Right Foot: *(page 19)*
1. footprint 2. footnote 3. footsore 4. underfoot 5. footwear 6. footman
7. football 8. footwork 9. foothill 10. footstool 11. tenderfoot 12. hotfoot
13. footstep 14. footbridge

"Hands" - on Riddles: *(page 20)*
Answers may vary.

Body Language: *(page 21)*
1. only a few people
3. very thin
5. many people can think of more ideas
7. begin correctly
9. very expensive
11. the person inside you
13. to have a disagreement

2. be prepared
4. make up your mind, determined
6. cannot see it so you don't think about it
8. almost dead
10. bottom of the stairs
12. stubborn, determined
14. constantly giving

An Unemployed Skeleton: *(page 22)*
Answers may vary.

Employee Application Form: *(page 23)*
Answers may vary.

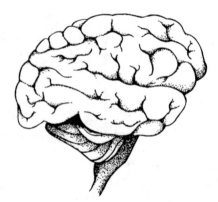

The Brain

Job Description: *(page 24)*
Answers may vary.

The Centers of the Brain: *(page 25)*
Answers may vary.

Does This Make "Sense"?: *(page 26)*

monocle - an eyeglass for one eye

echolocation - a radar-like system or mechanism of orientation in the sensory organs of certain mammals, such as bats or whales, by which they translate their own echoes into directional signals that permit them to avoid obstacles in their path

friction - a rubbing of one object against another, such as a hand against a hand

optometrist - a person skilled in examining the eyes and prescribing eyeglasses

iris - the colored part of the eye around the pupil; it controls the amount of light let in

cochlea - a spiral cavity of the inner ear; contains the nerve endings that transmit sound impulses along the auditory nerve

redolent - having a pleasant smell

ambrosia - something especially pleasing to the taste and smell

sonar - any device or system using the reflection of sound waves

hors d'oeuvre - food served before a meal to stimulate the appetite; appetizers

coarse - rough to the touch; not fine

aroma - sweet, spicy smell; distinctive fragrance or flavor

texture - the structure of something made or woven; makeup of the object

acoustic - having to do with the sense or the organs of hearing

retina - a layer of cells at the back of the eyeball which is sensitive to light and receives the images of things looked at

nasal - of, in, or from the nose

olfactory - having to do with smelling; organ for smelling

palatable - pleasing or agreeable to the taste

bitter - having a sharp, harsh, unpleasant taste

smooth - not rough or bumpy

spongy - having an open porous structure, full of holes

sour - not sweet; bitter, strong taste

pungent - sharply affecting the organs of smell and taste

sweet - pleasant taste or smell

noise - loud or harsh sound

crashing - a falling, hitting, or breaking sound

spicy - flavored with spice; sharp and fragrant

rough - not smooth; not level; uneven

musty - damp, moldy smell

odor - smell, fragrance, perfume, aroma

flashing - a sudden, brief light or flame

delicious - very pleasing to taste or smell

Touch - friction, coarse, texture, smooth, spongy, rough

Taste - ambrosia, hors d'oeuvre, palatable, bitter, sour, delicious, spicy, sweet

Sight - monocle, optometrist, iris, retina, flashing

Hearing - echolocation, cochlea, sonar, acoustic, crashing, noise

Smell - redolent, aroma, nasal, olfactory, pungent, musty, odor

Brain Bogglers: *(page 29)*

1. $8 - \dfrac{8}{8}$
2. 1 quarter, 5 dimes, 4 nickels, 5 pennies
3. 123 - 45 - 67 + 89 + 0 = 100
4. the 15
5. 11 jockeys, 15 horses
6. ◁◁

Capitalizing on Brains: *(page 30)*

1. The brain is divided into three sections — the cerebrum, the cerebellum, and the medulla.
2. The human brain is grayish-pink in color and weighs about 1.4 kilograms (three pounds).
3. The cerebrum weighs the most, totaling 85 percent of the 1.4 kilograms (three pounds).
4. Shielding the brain from hard blows are hard bones called the cranium.
5. The brain is at its full weight by the time a person is six years old.

"Brainy" Words: *(page 31)*

1. brainwash
2. brainwave
3. brainpan
4. brainchild
5. brainstorm
6. brain drain
7. brainless
8. brainy
9. brain teaser
10. brain fever

Great Minds: *(page 32)*

Answers may vary.

Brain Teasers: *(page 32)*

1.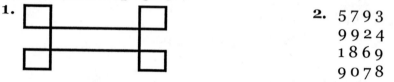

2. 5 7 9 3
   9 9 2 4
   1 8 6 9
   9 0 7 8

Good "Sense" Writing: *(page 33)*

Answers may vary.

The Circulatory System

The Heart - The Living Pump: *(page 34)*

chambers, auricle, ventricle, carbon dioxide, oxygen, bluish, red, vessel, aorta, cycle

"Heart" - y Words: *(page 36)*

1. heartily
2. heartfelt
3. hearty
4. hearth
5. heartburn
6. heartsick
7. heartless
8. heart-shaped
9. heartbroken
10. heart beat
11. heartworm
12. heartstrings

"Heart" - y Pioneers: *(page 37)*

Answers may vary.

Take Heart: *(page 37)*

Answers may vary.

Words From the Heart: *(page 38)*

heartache, heartbeat, heartbroken, heartburn, heartfelt, heartland, heartless, heartsick, heartstrings, hearty

heartache - great sorrow or grief; deep pain
heartbeat - pulsation of the heart; expansion and contraction of the heart
heartbroken - crushed by sorrow or grief; broken-hearted
heartburn - burning feeling in the chest and throat
heartfelt - very deeply felt; sincere, genuine, earnest

heartland - any area or region that is the centre of a country, institution or industry

heartless - without kindness or sympathy; unfeeling; cruel; callous

heartsick - sick at heart; very depressed; very unhappy

heartstrings - the deepest feelings; strongest affections; the tendons or nerves thought to support the heart

hearty - warm and friendly; genuine; sincere

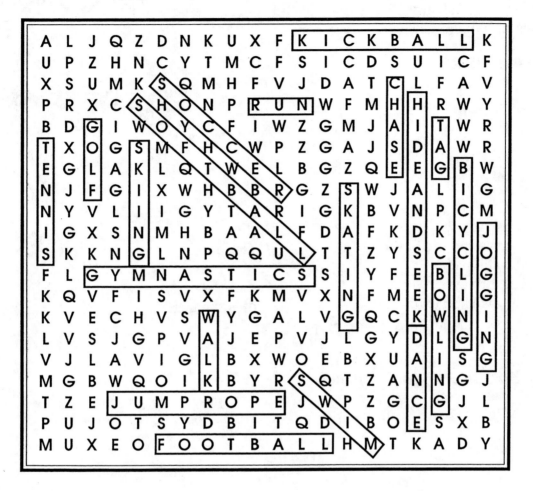

Exercise Word Search: *(page 39)*

Expressions of the Heart: *(page 40)*

3, 9, 1, 6, 7, 2, 10, 4, 8, 5, 15, 11, 13, 14, 12

The Muscular System

Muscles - Your Body's Movers: *(page 41)*
Answers may vary.

Muscles Versus Bones: *(page 41)*
Answers may vary.

Muscle Malady: *(page 42)*

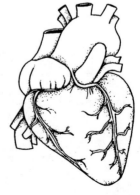

Answers may vary.

Order, Order: *(page 42)*
1. cardiac, cartilage, cells, connective, contract
2. facial, feelings, fibers, flesh, frown
3. markings, messages, motor, movers, muscles
4. skeletal, stomach, striped, strong, structure
5. tendon, thousands, threadlike, trunk, twined
6. vein, vessels, vigorous, vitamins, voluntary

Steroids: *(page 43)*
Answers may vary.

Let's Face It: *(page 43)*
Answers may vary.

The Hulk: *(page 44)*
Answers may vary.

Getting the "Gist" of It: *(page 45)*
1. studies muscles
2. studies the eye
3. studies nerves and the brain
4. studies bones
5. studies the stomach
6. studies tissues of the body
7. studies the kidneys
8. studies the ears, throat, and nose
9. studies the skin and hair
10. studies the heart

The Teeth

The Inside Story on Teeth: *(page 46)*
1. enamel 2. incisors 3. cuspids 4. bicuspids 5. molars, twelve
6. decay 7. plaque 8. cavities 9. brush, floss 10. dentist

Parts of a Tooth

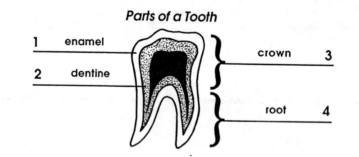

Primary Teeth

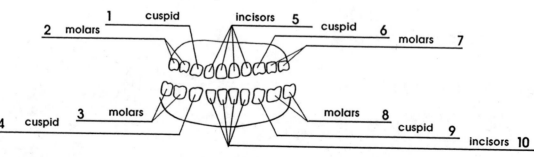

The Whole Tooth: *(page 47)*
Dental Health Quiz: *(page 48)*
Answers may vary.

My Wobbly Tooth: *(page 49)*
Answers may vary.

Toothy Alliteration: *(page 49)*
Answers may vary.

Brush Up on Toothbrushes!: *(page 50)*
Answers may vary.

Toothbrush to the Rescue: *(page 50)*
Answers may vary.

The Tooth Fairy: *(page 51)*
Answers may vary.

Plaque Attack: *(page 52)*
Answers may vary.

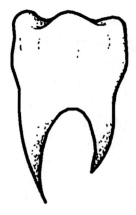

Say Cheese!: *(page 52)*
Answers may vary.

Story Starters: *(page 53)*
Answers may vary.

A Visit to the Dentist: *(page 54)*
Answers may vary.

Safety Rules: *(page 54)*
Answers may vary.

The Respiratory System

How We Breathe: *(page 55)*
nose, pharynx, larynx, trachea, bronchial, lungs, oxygen, carbon dioxide, breathing, inhalation, bronchus, trunk, bronchioles, alveoli, heart, cells, exhalation, contraction, diaphragm

Labeling a Diagram: *(page 56)*

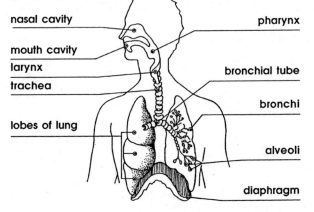

Respiratory Scramble: *(page 57)*

1. bronchial tube   2. nose   3. trachea   4. bronchiole   5. diaphragm
6. lungs   7. alveoli   8. epiglottis   9. pharynx   10. larynx

Catch Your Breath Part A: *(page 58)*

1. common cold   2. allergy   3. phlegm   4. tuberculosis   5. emphysema
6. asthma   7. bronchitis   8. pneumonia   9. humidifier   10. virus

Catch Your Breath Part B: *(page 60)*

Answers may vary.

Voyage to the Lungs: *(page 61)*

1. nose, mouth   2. lungs, cilia   3. diaphragm   4. throat, larynx   5. trachea
6. bronchi   7. alveoli

In and Out: *(page 62)*

1. The percentage of carbon dioxide inhaled is 0.04 percent. The percentage of carbon dioxide exhaled is four percent. Exhaled air has a higher percentage of carbon dioxide.
2. The amount of nitrogen in inhaled and exhaled air 78 percent. No, the percentage of nitrogen in inhaled and exhaled air does not differ.
3. Inhaled air contains 21 percent oxygen. Exhaled air contains sixteen percent oxygen. Therefore, five percent of the oxygen inhaled remains in the body.

The Digestive System

How Our Food is Digested: *(page 63)*

calories, digestion, gastrointestinal, alimentary, saliva, esophagus, muscles, peristalsis, stomach, gastric, intestine, chyme, pancreas, liver, bile, gall bladder, bloodstream, undigested, large, waste, rectum, solid, liquid

Labeling a Diagram: *(page 65)*

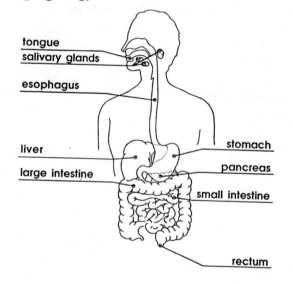

tongue
salivary glands
esophagus
liver
large intestine
stomach
pancreas
small intestine
rectum

Can You Stomach This?: *(page 66)*

1. d   2. f   3. h   4. a   5. c   6. i   7. b   8. g   9. e

Word Search: *(page 67)*

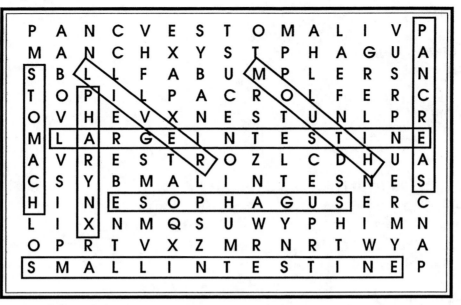

```
P  A  N  C  V  E  S  T  O  M  A  L  I  V  P
M  A  N  C  H  X  Y  S  T  P  H  A  G  U  A
S  B  L  I  F  A  B  U  M  P  L  E  R  S  N
T  O  P  I  L  P  A  C  R  O  L  F  E  R  C
O  V  H  E  V  X  N  E  S  T  U  N  L  P  R
M  L  A  R  G  E  I  N  T  E  S  T  I  N  E
A  V  R  E  S  T  R  O  Z  L  C  D  H  U  A
C  S  Y  B  M  A  L  I  N  T  E  S  N  E  S
H  I  N  E  S  O  P  H  A  G  U  S  E  R  C
L  I  X  N  M  Q  S  U  W  Y  P  H  I  M  N
O  P  R  T  V  X  Z  M  R  N  R  T  W  Y  A
S  M  A  L  L  I  N  T  E  S  T  I  N  E  P
```

Facts to Digest: *(page 68)*

1. Enzyme is a complex organic substance that promotes chemical changes in other substances
2. Chyme is food mixed with stomach chemicals
3. Peristalsis is a muscular movement
4. Bile is a secretion of the liver that aids digestion
5. Bolus is a lump of chewed food
6. Pepsin is a digestive enzyme secreted by the stomach
7. Metabolize means to change substances chemically within a living organism in order to release useful energy

Down the Hatch: *(page 71)*

Answers may vary.

Nutrition

Nutrition Squad: *(page 72)*

Answers may vary.

Nutri-Wise: *(page 74)*

Answers may vary.

Pumping Iron: *(page 75)*

Answers may vary.

Food Trivia: *(page 76)*

1. false   2. false   3. false   4. true   5. false   6. false   7. true   8. true
9. true   10. true

Food For Thought: *(page 77)*

1. 425 calories
2. cup whole wheat flour, cup wheat germ, cup all-purpose flour, tbsp. baking powder, $\frac{3}{8}$ tbsp. salt, egg beaten, $\frac{1}{8}$ cups skim milk, $1\frac{1}{4}$ tbsp. vegetable oil $\frac{1}{2}$
3. 120 bags; 3\frac{1}{2}$.00 $\frac{5}{8}$

4. Answers may vary.

5. $6.26; $13.74

Sensible Snacking: *(page 79)*
Answers may vary.

Who Am I?: *(page 80)*
1. spinach   **2.** corn   **3.** potato   **4.** okra   **5.** celery or artichoke
6. asparagus   **7.** string beans   **8.** lettuce   **9.** bananas   **10.** carrot top

Food Label Study: *(page 81)*
Answers may vary.

How Many Ways Can You Say Eat?: *(page 82)*
Answer may vary.

"Dairy" Good: *(page 83)*
kelp, locust beans, Irish moss, eggs, beet, cane, corn syrup, dextrose, vanilla beans, pineapple, strawberries, cacao, beans, bananas

What's "New" - tritional in Foods?: *(page 84)*
Answers may vary.

Out to Lunch: *(page 85)*
Answers may vary.

The Cholesterol Question: *(page 86)*
Answers may vary.